Issuing Divine
RESTRAINING
ORDERS *from*
the Courts of Heaven

Issuing Divine

RESTRAINING
ORDERS *from*
the Courts of Heaven

RESTRICTING AND REVOKING
THE PLANS OF THE ENEMY

DR. FRANCIS MYLES
WITH ROBERT HENDERSON

DESTINY IMAGE® PUBLISHERS, INC.
P.O. Box 310, Shippensburg, PA 17257-0310
"Promoting Inspired Lives."

This book and all other Destiny Image and Destiny Image Fiction books are available at Christian bookstores and distributors worldwide.

Cover design by Eileen Rockwell

For more information on foreign distributors, call 717-532-3040.

Reach us on the Internet: www.destinyimage.com.

ISBN 13 TP: 978-0-7684-4558-9

ISBN 13 eBook: 978-0-7684-4559-6

ISBN 13 HC: 978-0-7684-4561-9

ISBN 13 LP: 978-0-7684-4560-2

For Worldwide Distribution, Printed in the U.S.A.

1 2 3 4 5 6 7 8 / 23 22 21 20 19

Dedication

The Lord gave the word: great was the company of those that published it (Psalm 68:11 KJV).

I T has been said that great projects are never the work of one man but the collective effort of a team that shares a common destiny. I want to give a heartfelt "God bless you" to the following brothers and sisters for making the publishing of this book a reality. May God give you a tremendous harvest for every person who will be transformed by the truths contained within this book.

Carmela Real Myles, my best friend, wife, and partner in the business of advancing the Kingdom of God.

To my spiritual children at Lovefest Church International whose zeal for my apostolic assignment energizes me daily and who also helped me authenticate the spiritual technology contained in this book.

Kimberly Sparrow (my zealous spiritual daughter). Thank you, Kimberly, for believing in the message that I am called to bring to the Body of Christ. Thanks a million times for taking time to help me proofread this book.

Contents

Preface

I N this book, I want to talk to you about an important aspect of the Courts of Heaven. The Lord began to speak to me about this aspect of operating in the Courts of Heaven a while back. There are times when God gives His children an experience before He gives them the revelation behind the experience. This is usually the way the Lord works with me. The Holy Spirit usually gives me a real-life or prophetic experience to trigger my very inquisitive theological mind. The Lord knows that He created me like a hound dog—once I sniff the scent of a special divine revelation on the horizon, I never rest until God unpacks the revelation to me. I usually find myself saying, "Lord, what was that?" In response to my deep cry for answers, the Lord usually begins to *reverse engineer the revelation that my prophetic experience is controlled by.*

It's important for followers of Christ to know the ways of the Spirit and not just be comfortable with the acts of God. The Bible tells us that Moses knew God's ways, but the people of Israel only knew His acts. The people of Israel could talk about His miracles (acts), but Moses could perform them repeatedly because he knew the ways of the Spirit. If we knew the ways of the Spirit, then we could relive most of our prophetic experiences as we follow the Lord Jesus.

In this life-changing book, I want to talk to you about *Issuing Divine Restraining Orders from the Courts of Heaven*. In this book I am going to explain the purpose of "restraining orders" from a natural standpoint within our earthly judicial systems. After this I will upgrade our conversation to the subject of defining "divine restraining orders" from a spiritual standpoint because they are an important aspect of operating from the Courts of Heaven. The Holy Spirit also showed me that there are many children of God who are failing to land or fulfill their God-given destiny here on earth because they're in direct violation of divine restraining orders the Lord imposed upon their life and calling. Like Samson of old, many of God's children have "cut their hair of consecration" on the lap of the Delilah spirit. They continue to languish in a cesspool of depression and an unending sense of frustration while the destiny God promised them becomes more unattainable. Like Samson of old, we need to repent for violating a restraining order of the Courts of Heaven. If we don't repent, the devil will continue to have legal standing before the Courts of Heaven to resist the actualization of our destiny here on earth.

Let me ask you a couple of questions: Have you ever had a restraining order issued against you? Have you ever filed a judicial petition for a restraining order against someone you felt posed a danger to you physically? Do you know someone or an ex-spouse who went to jail because of violating a court's restraining or protective order? My questions are intentional because I wish to make a point—restraining or protective orders are an integral part of all earthly judicial systems! That said, how can the highest courts of appeal in the universe, the Courts of Heaven, fail to have their own restraining or protective orders?

> *Jesus answered and said to him, "Most assuredly, I say to you, unless one is born again, he cannot see the kingdom of God" (John 3:3).*

We must not forget that we are saved (born again) to enter the Kingdom of God. Our heavenly Father is the sovereign ruler of the greatest Kingdom in the entire universe. The Kingdom is not a congregation; it's a real government with a king, country (heaven), military (angels), and citizens. Like all legitimate governments, the Kingdom of God has a judicial branch of the government of God. I am very grateful to my dear covenant brother Apostle Robert Henderson whom God is using worldwide to teach the Body of Christ about *Operating in the Courts of Heaven*. His books, among others, are helping the global Body of Christ understand how to cooperate with the judicial branch of the government of God's Kingdom. It is my heartfelt prayer that this book, *Issuing Divine Restraining Orders from the Courts of Heaven*, will add to the arsenal of books that God is using to seize every legal right and avenue Satan has been using to steal, kill, and destroy (see John 10:10) the destinies of God's children here on earth.

Yours for Kingdom advancement,

—Dr. Francis Myles
Author, *The Order of Melchizedek*
Senior Pastor, Lovefest Church International
Francismyles.com

Chapter 1

OPERATING *from the* Heavenly Courtroom

by Robert Henderson

RESTRAINING orders are a common thing within our judicial system in America. Wikipedia defines a restraining or protective order as being "used by a court to protect a person, business, company, establishment, or entity, and the general public, in a situation involving alleged domestic violence, harassment, stalking, or sexual assault."[1] Even though the terminology *restraining* or *protective order* isn't used in Scripture we can definitely recognize it as being there. There are many instances where the Lord and His host of heaven shielded and protected those belonging to Him. A restraining or protective order is legal in nature. Therefore it requires judicial activity to see it implemented. This involves the Courts of Heaven. It is possible to see the Lord as Judge set in place a restraining or protective order that will not allow the devil a right to interfere, hurt, destroy, or touch that which belongs to Him. Before we can fully understand a restraining order in the Spirit realm we must have a concept of the Courts of Heaven and their operation.

The Courts of Heaven are a very real place that we as believers have access into. In these Courts, we can petition the Lord as our Judge to render these restraining orders to set boundaries around our lives. One of the places the Courts of Heaven are seen in is Daniel 7:9-10.

> I watched till thrones were put in place, and the Ancient of Days was seated; His garment was white as snow, and the hair of His head was like pure wool. His throne was a fiery flame, its wheels a burning fire; a fiery stream issued and came forth from before Him. A thousand thousands ministered to Him; ten thousand times ten thousand stood before Him. The court was seated, and the books were opened.

We see Daniel having an encounter and a vision from the Lord. We know this is true because he says that he "watched" as these things were occurring. The end result of what he saw was the Court of Heaven coming to order and being ready to exercise its authority over things in heaven and in earth. The things mentioned here are some of the activities of this Court. We see thrones plural being set in place. These are seats of government that both heavenly and earthly creatures/people sit in. We know there are 24 elders, who are heavenly beings, sitting in thrones around the Throne of God. Revelation 4:4 chronicles these elders and their place in the Courts of Heaven:

> Around the throne were twenty-four thrones, and on the thrones I saw twenty-four elders sitting, clothed in white robes; and they had crowns of gold on their heads.

These sit in a judicial council around the Throne of God. They along with the Lord Himself would seem to hear the cases presented to the Courts of Heaven. They would, it appears, have input into the decisions rendered from the Courts of Heaven concerning things in earth and heaven. There is, however, also those who are yet in the earth who sit on thrones or seats of government in the spirit realm. For instance, Proverbs 20:8 tells us of kings who sit on thrones and the power, authority, and influence they wield.

> *A king who sits on the throne of judgment scatters all evil with his eyes.*

A king does not just speak of someone who naturally rules a nation. It also speaks of those who have obtained and been positioned by the Lord in the spirit world. They have such a place in the realm of the spirit while they are yet living and functioning in the natural that just a look of their eyes scatters evil. This would be the authority and *seats of government* or *thrones* that God would grant us access into. This is what Jesus meant in Revelation 3:21 when He spoke of us sitting with Him on His Throne.

> *To him who overcomes I will grant to sit with Me on My throne, as I also overcame and sat down with My Father on His throne.*

This is not speaking of the afterlife. This is speaking of a place in the spirit realm we can occupy today. When we overcome the pull of the flesh, the emotions of the natural, and other human struggles, we qualify to sit with Him on His Throne. From this place in the spiritual dimensions we can be a part of the operation of the Courts of Heaven. I think it is interesting that Daniel *watched* as these thrones were set in place. For the full decisions of the Court of Heaven to occur there must be those in heaven in their thrones, but also those of us in earth in our thrones. We can then become a part of the activity and renderings of the Court of Heaven.

Another thing that Daniel saw was *the Throne* of God. This is where judicial decisions are made that order life in heaven and in earth. God as Judge of all sits on this throne. Hebrews 12:23 proclaims this title over the Lord.

> *To the general assembly and church of the firstborn who are registered in heaven, to God the Judge of all, to the spirits of just men made perfect.*

His Throne is a throne of judicial activity. Psalm 89:14 tells us righteousness and justice are the foundational structure of God's Throne. In other words, this is what makes God's Throne so powerful. True righteousness and justice flow from the Lord because this is who He is upon His Throne.

> *Righteousness and justice are the foundation of Your throne; mercy and truth go before Your face.*

In the midst of His Throne being one of righteousness and justice it also releases mercy and truth. I am so very thankful for this. Out of the righteous realm and just dimension of who God is, He also is merciful, kind, and gracious. Mercy and truth go before His face. God extends mercy to those who repent at His truth. When we respond in affirmation to His truth and seek to order our lives accordingly, His mercy is manifested upon us.

As with any Court, the Court of Heaven issues verdicts that are to establish a pattern in life. When a Judge decrees a verdict it can change a life. So it is with the Lord as our Judge from His Court. I believe this is what is being referred to when it declares "*a fiery stream issued and came forth before Him.*" These are verdicts and decisions coming from the Throne of God. When God as Judge issues verdicts, they are as a fire going forth from Him. Psalm 97:2-3 shows that the righteous judgments of the Lord are as a fire going before Him to consume His enemies.

> *Clouds and darkness surround Him; righteousness and justice are the foundation of His throne. A fire goes before Him, and burns up His enemies round about.*

When the Lord renders decisions from His Courts/Throne, it is as a fire destroying His enemies. All that would be standing in the way of His desire in the earth is removed because of a verdict being set in place. This is what happens when the Court of Heaven is in operation. We actually see this in Daniel 7:25-27. In these verses we see the antichrist spirit in operation in the earth. It is seeking to work the diabolical plan of the satanic.

> *He shall speak pompous words against the Most High, shall persecute the saints of the Most High, and shall intend to change times and law. Then the saints shall be given into his hand for a time and times and half a time. But the court shall be seated, and they shall take away his dominion, to consume and destroy it forever. Then the kingdom and dominion, and the greatness of the kingdoms under the whole heaven, shall be given to the people, the saints of the Most High. His kingdom is an everlasting kingdom, and all dominions shall serve and obey Him.*

The "he" in these verses is speaking of what we would call the antichrist. This is the spirit that is operating in the earth, fighting against the intent and will of God. It presently is having great effect in the nations of the world. This is why we see such outlandish ideas taking hold across the globe. They literally for most of us would seem illogical and even insane. In many nations, men are being permitted to use women's restroom facilities. All because they "feel" like a woman. Children are being taught how to be "homosexuals" in school. Transgender people are being invited into schools to influence children and bring their idea of what culture should be. These and many other activities are contending against traditional standards set by the church and God's Word in culture. It is as if anything related to God and His standards is being challenged as irrelevant and archaic. This is the antichrist spirit functioning to take over nations. First John 4:3 tells us that the antichrist spirit is already operating in the world.

> *And every spirit that does not confess that Jesus Christ has come in the flesh is not of God. And this is the spirit of the Antichrist, which you have heard was coming, and is now already in the world.*

Any spirit that denies Jesus and His effect in the natural world is antichrist. It denies Jesus' right to influence individuals, life, and cultures. It wants to set things up after its own rules and ideas. We saw that one of its purposes is to *"change times and laws."* In other words, it wants to alter the standards society has been founded upon. Everything comes into question. We are told that in the midst of this environment, the people of God come under persecution and are tormented by this spirit and its philosophies. There is, however, a solution. *The Court is seated and takes away his dominion to consume and destroy it forever.* In other words, a verdict and decision from the Court of Heaven revokes the right of this spirit to operate and frees culture from its effects. The result is the people of God brought out of a place of defeat and into a place of dominion. This all occurs because of a verdict from God's Court. He sends forth a fiery stream and burns up all His enemies. The power and authority that flows from the Court of Heaven is supreme! This means we can stand before His Court and see verdicts rendered that alter life on the planet. That which would threaten us is revoked and removed, because God sets a restraining and protective order in place. This actually happened in the days of Job. It is said in Job 1:8-10 that God had set a *hedge* about Job.

> *Then the Lord said to Satan, "Have you considered My servant Job, that there is none like him on the earth, a blameless and upright man, one who fears God and shuns evil?"*
>
> *So Satan answered the Lord and said, "Does Job fear God for nothing? Have You not made a hedge around him, around his household, and around all that he has on every side? You have blessed the work of his hands, and his possessions have increased in the land."*

The word *hedge* is the Hebrew word *suwk*. It means to shut in for protection or restraint. Satan was complaining that Job only served God because of how blessed he was. This blessing was because there was a restraining and protective order in the spirit realm that would not allow Satan to touch him. When we walk before the Lord, from the Courts of Heaven God will set a *hedge or restraining and protective order in place.* This will prohibit the attacks of the devil and will allow only the blessing of God in our lives. The Bible actually tells us what had allowed this restraining order to be in place. It tells us what Job had done that allowed God to order this. Job 1:8 shows God's opinion of Job that would have caused the Lord to set this restraining order in place for him.

> *Then the Lord said to Satan, "Have you considered My servant Job, that there is none like him on the earth, a blameless and upright man, one who fears God and shuns evil?"*

There are at least six qualities that God speaks of concerning Job that allowed the Court of Heaven to set up a restraining/protective order over him. The first is God calls Job His *servant*. This means a bond-servant. In other words, Job had entered into being God's bond-slave. Exodus 21:5-6 shows us the idea of one who had to serve another for six years because of his debt. At the end of the six years as he entered the seventh he could go free. He could, however, at this point make a choice to *stay* and remain a servant in his master's house. If he chose this, he would forever be the servant of this man. He is now no longer a servant but a bond-slave.

> *But if the servant plainly says, "I love my master, my wife, and my children; I will not go out free," then his master shall bring him to the judges. He shall also bring him to the door, or to the doorpost, and his master shall pierce his ear with an awl; and he shall serve him forever.*

This is a picture of what happens to us. We begin serving Jesus because of His power to forgive and deliver us from a debt we could never pay. However, in the process of serving Him, we fall into love with Him and His house. The result is we do not want to go free. Our heart has now been taken captive by His love and life. We desire to be His bond-slave. We are then *marked* with a pierced ear. This speaks of our ear being *opened* to hear. The mark of a bond-slave is an ear to hear and a heart to obey expressly. We now belong to another. This is who Job was. He being a bond-slave of the Lord had allowed God to set a restraining order around him and all his family. The result was a life that was untouchable to the devil until Satan built a case that caused God to remove it. The good news is that the divine restraining/protective order was in finality put back in place.

The second thing that allowed God to set this restraining order was *there was none like him* in all the earth. This means Job did what others wouldn't do. His commitment was above and beyond the norm of his day. Sometimes we think we can have what someone else has without meeting the requirements they have met. This normally is not true. If we want the life, power, protection, safety, prosperity, and glory someone walks in, it will cost us the price they have paid. Job had lived a life separated to the Lord and dedicated to Him and His purposes. The result was a restraining/protective order under which he was blessed and empowered.

The third thing Job did that allowed this restraining order to be in force was he was *blameless*. This word in the Hebrew is *tam*. It means to be complete but also means to be *coupled together*. Job walked as a mature man before God because of his joining to the Lord. His power to please God was found in his union with the Lord. This means Job walked in an intimate relationship with God that God honored. It was the passion of God to protect and bless Job because of the intimacy they shared. If we are to walk under the restraining order of God for us and our families, we must walk in union, intimacy, and closeness with the Lord. This means times of fellowship and communion are essential. These times spent developing a nearness to the Lord will produce protection from Him that will allow us to flourish and manifest the blessed life.

A fourth secret that Job walked in was he was *upright*. This word in the Hebrew means to *be straight*. Many of us would have heard the phrase, "*He's as straight as an arrow.*" This always is speaking of the integrity and character of someone. They are being touted as being one who is impeccable in the dealing of their life. Job was a man who had no compromise in his life. The result was a life under the restraining/protective order of God. So often it is the little compromises of our life that allow the devil the legal right to bring hurt and harm to us. We must be *straight*. The *little* compromises we allow in our lives can arrange *big* opportunities for the devil's devouring. May we walk before the Lord in an uncompromising way that allows His restraining orders to work in our behalf.

The fifth key to Job's living under the restraining hand of God was he *feared God*. Of course the fear of the Lord is a major reason for how and where Job walked. If you boil down the fear of the Lord, I believe it is to love righteousness and hate evil. When we fear God, we carry a passion to love what He loves and to hate what He hates. Psalm 45:6-7 tells us this is the reason the pleasure of the Father was upon Jesus.

> *Your throne, O God, is forever and ever; a scepter of righteousness is the scepter of Your kingdom. You love righteousness and hate wickedness; therefore God, Your God, has anointed You with the oil of gladness more than Your companions.*

Notice that as a result of loving righteousness and hating wickedness, there was an anointing of gladness on Jesus more than His brothers or companions. When we walk in the fear of the Lord, it doesn't birth a living in terror. It in fact does just the opposite. It grants us a life of surety, confidence, joy, and gladness. As Job walked before the Lord in the fear of God, he lived this life. The result was the restraining and protective hand of God on him and all he loved.

The last thing I will mention that characterized Job and his life in the protective and safe place of the Lord was he *shunned evil*. This word in the Hebrew means to *turn off*. In other words, Job *turned off* the pull of evil or the temptation that would have led him astray.

When Satan would come with a temptation to seek to pull him away, Job would *turn it off* or say no to it and allow it no influence over him. How we need to learn to do this. We must set our minds on things above and not of this earth (see Col. 3:2). We must allow our minds to be occupied with the Lord and His passions and not the lust of the flesh or the desires of a carnal mind. When we make these choices daily or even hourly or in moments, we are *turning off* the opportunity of evil against us. This is the kind of life Job lived. The result was a restraining order from heaven on his behalf. We know Satan built a case against Job and this order was lifted for a while.

However, because of Job's faithfulness and God's favor and kindness it was restored. Job got back double all that was lost. God restored the protective/restraining order from the Courts of Heaven in Job's life. We can have it too. May the grace of God work mightily in us that the Courts of Heaven will have the rights to render for us the restraining and protecting presence of God over our life. We will live under the canopy of His glory that no demon or devil can penetrate or access. We will walk in the light and glory of His presence and power!

Life Application
S E C T I O N

Memory Verse

Clouds and darkness surround Him; righteousness and justice are the foundation of His throne. A fire goes before Him, and burns up His enemies round about (Psalm 97:2-3).

Reflections

1. Name one reason that caused God to place a divine restraining/ protective order over Job's life?

_____

_____

_____

_____

_____

2. What was Satan's primary accusation against Job?

_____

_____

_____

_____

_____

Chapter 2

The PRINCIPLE
of Divine Restraint

God will never use a man His Spirit can never restrain!
— Francis Myles

ONE of the most powerful Kingdom principles for working with God and maintaining spiritual authority is a foundational principle I call the *principle of divine restraint*. It would seem to me that this principle is at the heart of God's dealings with mankind. The principle of divine restraint was self-evident in the life of the Lord Jesus Christ and we'll examine this fact before I conclude this chapter. *The principle of divine restraint is the foundation for the whole subject of issuing divine restraining orders.* We will fail to appreciate why issuing divine restraining orders is such an important aspect of operating in the Courts of Heaven if we fail to understand the role the principle of divine restraint plays in the government of the Kingdom of God.

Divine Restraint:
The Key to Spiritual Authority

*Then the Lord God took the man and put him in the garden
of Eden to tend and keep it. And the Lord God commanded
the man, saying, "Of every tree of the garden you may
freely eat; but of the tree of the knowledge of good and evil
you shall not eat, for in the day that you eat of it you shall
surely die"* (Genesis 2:15-17).

Divine restraint is the key to spiritual authority. As God is the
ultimate Authority, we will never understand natural or spiritual
authority without looking to God. God's favorite title is "Father" or
"Abba." *Abba* is a Greek word that means "Source, Provider, Sustainer or Foundation." Abba means "Source," so God is the Source of
everything. Consequently, Father God is the source of all *authority* in
heaven and on earth. Abba also means "Sustainer," so it means that
Father God is the sustainer of any kind of authority, both natural and
spiritual. Abba also means "Provider," so it means that Father God is
the One who provides us with authority, both natural and spiritual.
This explains why mankind will be held accountable for how we all
responded to both spiritual and natural authority. This is due to the
fact that authority is an ordinance of God (see Rom. 13).

Finally, the word *Abba* also means "foundation." It means that
Father God is the foundation of any kind of authority, both natural
and spiritual. So it's safe to say that authority has God as its primary
foundation. This explains why Jesus said this to Pontius Pilate:

*You would have no authority over Me at all if it had not
been given to you from above. For this reason the sin and*

guilt of the one who handed Me over to you is greater [than your own] (John 19:11 AMP).

In my study of Scripture, I discovered something really amazing about authority. I discovered by revelation that it's impossible to have authority or retain it without being under a *restraining principle*. This restraining principle follows authority like a man's shadow. Let us break down Genesis 2:15-17 to understand how God embedded this restraining principle in Adam's authority over the Garden of Eden and the entire animal kingdom. The expression, *"Then the Lord God took the man and put him in the garden of Eden to tend and keep it,"* establishes Father God as the Source of Adam's authority and the reason that God gave him that authority. Adam needed authority in order to cultivate and manage the Garden of Eden.

However, here comes the critical *restraining principle*:

> And the Lord God **commanded** the man, saying, "Of every tree of the garden you may freely eat; **but of the tree of the knowledge of good and evil you shall not eat, for in the day that you eat of it you shall surely die."**

Before the Lord taught me about the *principle of divine restraint*, I was among those who asked the question, "Why did God put the tree of the knowledge of good and evil in the Garden of Eden knowing that Adam might be tempted to eat from it?" Frankly, I thought my question was brilliant. When the Lord showed me that all authority requires a restraining principle, it's like a light bulb went on inside of me.

Think about this: If you have a housemaid and you give her this instruction: "Do not let anybody into the house while I am away," what have you done to your housemaid? You have just given her authority over anybody who wants access to your house while you are away. In that instant, your housemaid has more authority over your house than your biological mother and father! Obviously, the housemaid loses that authority the moment you return. However, while you are away the *restraining principle* that you put her under gives her *tremendous authority* over who has access to your house. I hope you're catching the picture.

The Lord said to me, "Francis, there was no way I could give Adam authority over the Garden of Eden without putting him under a *restraining principle.*" Adam's authority over the Garden of Eden was rooted in his ability to adhere to the restraining principle that God put him under. It's safe to say that it is the restraining principle that maintains and sustains authority. God did not hide the consequences for violating the restraining principle that was connected to Adam's authority over the Garden of Eden. God said, *"For in the day that you eat of it you shall surely die."* In other words, true spiritual authority dies or ends when the *divine* restraining principle is broken. It's important for us to understand the importance of the principle of divine restraint before we enter into the Courts of Heaven and begin to discuss the Kingdom judicial process for *issuing divine restraining orders from the Courts of Heaven.*

Samson's Tragic Fall!

Now there was a certain man from Zorah, of the family of the Danites, whose name was Manoah; and his wife was barren and had no children. And the Angel of the Lord appeared to the woman and said to her, "Indeed now, you are barren and have borne no children, but you shall conceive and bear a son. Now therefore, please be careful not to drink wine or similar drink, and not to eat anything unclean. For behold, you shall conceive and bear a son. And no razor shall come upon his head, for the child shall be a Nazirite to God from the womb; and he shall begin to deliver Israel out of the hand of the Philistines" (Judges 13:2-5).

One of the most tragic stories in the Bible, in my humble opinion, is the fall of the mighty Samson! Samson's tragic story brings to the forefront the critical importance of respecting the restraining order (principle) that God has placed upon our life. By all accounts, the story of Samson is a story about the supernatural.

First, his mother was barren. This means that it was impossible, biologically speaking, for her to conceive. This biological impossibility ended when an angel of the Lord appeared to her and told her she would be the mother of a deliverer. The angel declared to her that heaven had just opened her womb. However, the angel immediately placed her miraculous conception under a restraining principle or order. Here is what the angel told her: "Please be careful not to drink wine or similar drink, and not to eat anything unclean." This was the restraining order that would protect her pregnancy and guarantee the birth of her son. This means that it was not enough that heaven had opened her barren womb; she needed to couple that with adhering to the restraining order that the angel of the Lord had placed upon her life during the term of the pregnancy.

However, the angel was not yet finished giving her instructions. There was additional information about her "miracle baby" that would follow him throughout his life. The restraining order on the child's life was even more consequential than the shorter one the Lord had placed upon the mother's life for the duration of her pregnancy. Here is what the angel said about the boy:

> For behold, you shall conceive and bear a son. And no razor shall come upon his head, for the child shall be a Nazirite to God from the womb; and he shall begin to deliver Israel out of the hand of the Philistines.

The boy (Samson) was not allowed to shave his hair. This was the restraining principle that would be connected to his ability to deliver the people of Israel from the hands of the Philistines. The implication is obvious—violation of this divine restraining order by Samson would strip him of this supernatural power over the Philistines.

The Delilah Spirit!

One of the most surprising things about Samson is that even though he lived what most of us would consider an immoral lifestyle, he could still destroy the Philistines like they were nothing! This is both amazing and mind-boggling to me. Samson would have been an absolute failure in the church's "holiness class." He was always entangled in some sexual affair with a woman, but if the Philistines tried to attack Israel he could destroy these seasoned men of war with a jawbone of an ass! For the longest time, Samson's story offended my Pentecostal holiness sensibilities. "How could God use such an immoral man?" I asked.

However, when the Lord began to teach me about the restraining principle, that's when I understood Samson. The Lord showed me that Samson's supernatural strength was never connected to his sexual chastity; it was *connected to his hair*. As a Nazarite, his hair could never be cut, but the angel never said anything about his lifestyle with women. The divine restraining order was connected to his hair and not his lifestyle with women. However, Samson's love for women would eventually be his undoing. This is essentially the moral of the story—there is a lifestyle (holiness before the Lord) that can best protect the restraining order the Lord has placed upon our life and ministry.

> *Afterward it happened that he loved a woman in the Valley of Sorek, whose name was Delilah. And the lords of the Philistines came up to her and said to her, "Entice him, and find out where his great strength lies, and by what means we may overpower him, that we may bind him to afflict him; and every one of us will give you eleven hundred pieces of silver."*
>
> *So Delilah said to Samson, "Please tell me where your great strength lies, and with what you may be bound to afflict you"* (Judges 16:4-6).

I am convinced that Satan always assigns a "Delilah" to any man or woman of destiny. There is a "Delilah spirit" that wants to know the secret to your anointing. God overlooked Samson's multiple affairs and continued to use him mightily. Why? Samson had not yet violated the divine restraining order that the Courts of Heaven had imposed upon him as a judge in Israel. The Spirit of God continued to back him up with supernatural strength, but Delilah kept nagging him. The Delilah spirit is determined to discover the source of your strength in the Lord. One day she nagged him so much she wore him out. Why didn't he just leave her? He was addicted to her sexually. My dear brothers and sisters, the devil will wear you out until he discovers the restraining principle to which your spiritual gift is connected.

When he finds it, he will start tempting you to sell out! The devil knows that spiritual authority in God's Kingdom requires a restraining principle. Every person God uses mightily must be restrained in some way or the other. *This is because God cannot use a person He cannot restrain!*

> *Then she said to him, "How can you say, 'I love you,' when your heart is not with me? You have mocked me these three times, and have not told me where your great strength lies." And it came to pass, when she pestered him daily with her words and pressed him, so that his soul was vexed to death, that he told her all his heart, and said to her, "No razor has ever come upon my head, for I have been a Nazirite to God from my mother's womb. **If I am shaven, then my strength will leave me, and I shall become weak, and be like any other man"** (Judges 16:15-17).*

Samson should never have told her. If I were Samson's publicist I would have said, "Why did you expose the secret of your strength to a prostitute for hire?" The Bible says:

> *When Delilah saw that he had told her all his heart, she sent and called for the lords of the Philistines, saying, "Come up once more, for he has told me all his heart"* (Judges 16:18).

The Delilah spirit knows the moment you expose the secret of your strength in the Lord. This spirit quickly moves in to destroy you by tempting you to violate the divine restraining order that God imposed on your life and calling. All divine restraining orders are issued from the Courts of Heaven, so Satan knows that violation of such an order gives him solid legal ground to attack or destroy any child of God and their ministry. Satan knew that Samson was exposed and guilty. Satan knew that Samson was now guilty of "contempt of court" in the Courts of Heaven. I believe Satan quickly called for an emergency trial against Samson and scheduled a hearing with God. His evidence against Samson was rock solid, so the mantle of divine protection that was upon Samson was quickly removed. The devil had every legal right to move in and do with Samson as he pleased. The fact that the Philistines did not kill Samson when they finally got a hold of him means that Satan was never given the legal right to take Samson's life. I call this the amazing mercy of God!

> *And she said, "The Philistines are upon you, Samson!" So he awoke from his sleep, and said, "I will go out as before, at other times, and shake myself free!" But he did not know that the Lord had departed from him. Then the Philistines took him and put out his eyes, and brought him down to Gaza. They bound him with bronze fetters, and he became a grinder in the prison* (Judges 16:20-21).

Delilah shaved Samson's hair and then began to torment him. She called the Philistine lords to come and bind the great Samson. When they came, Samson tried to overpower them but tragically *the Lord had departed from him*. Since the divine restraining order that controlled his supernatural strength was violated, Samson was easy prey for the Philistines. The Philistines took out Samson's eyes and paraded him as a token of victory before their people. Samson was then moved to prison where he became a grinder of Philistine grain. How sad and tragic! But his hair would soon grow back, restoring the divine restraining order upon his life. What a merciful God we serve!

Divine Restraint in the Life of Jesus

*Then Jesus answered and said to them, "Most assuredly, I
say to you, the Son can do nothing of Himself, but what He
sees the Father do; for whatever He does, the Son also does
in like manner"* (John 5:19).

I want to close this chapter by showing you the active operation
of the *principle of divine restraint* in the life of the Lord Jesus Christ.
Jesus wasted no time in exposing the fact that this essential principle
lay at the heart of His life-changing earthly ministry. Let's hear Jesus
tell it: *"Most assuredly, I say to you, **the Son can do nothing** of Himself, **but what He sees the Father do**."* Jesus makes it clear that there
was a restraining principle or order on His life, ministry, and calling.
The expression *the Son can do nothing of Himself* points to Father God
as the Source of the Son's authority. This statement is followed by
another equally important statement, which describes the restraining
principle.

The "restraining principle or order" on the Son of God's ministry is
contained in the expression *the Son can do nothing of Himself, but what
He sees the Father do*. Wow! Jesus was very aware of this restraining
principle over His life. Even during His temptation during His famous
40-day fast (see Luke 4), Satan tried to free Jesus from the restraining
order that was upon His life. Every temptation of Satan (the Accuser)
was designed to *frustrate the restraining principle* that anchored the
authority of the Son of God on earth. Satan essentially tried to force
the Son of Man (Jesus) to act as though He was equal with God in
His substitutionary role as the slain lamb. Jesus never took the bait.
He knew that to be the perfect sacrifice He had to empty Himself of
being fully God so He could be "fully man" in His redemptive work.

> *When He came to the place, He said to them, "Pray that*
> *you may not enter into temptation." And He was with-*
> *drawn from them about a stone's throw, and He knelt down*
> *and prayed, saying, "Father, if it is Your will, take this*
> *cup away from Me; nevertheless not My will, but Yours,*
> *be done." Then an angel appeared to Him from heaven,*
> *strengthening Him. And being in agony, He prayed more*
> *earnestly. Then His sweat became like great drops of blood*
> *falling down to the ground. When He rose up from prayer,*
> *and had come to His disciples, He found them sleeping from*
> *sorrow* (Luke 22:40-45).

Even in the Garden of Gethsemane, Satan never gave up on tempting Jesus to violate the divine restraining order that His Father, the Righteous Judge, had placed upon His life as Savior of the world. In the Garden of Gethsemane, the Holy Spirit showed me that the Lord Jesus went through the most difficult fight He ever had during His time on earth to maintain the divine restraining order on His life. Luke's account shows us the fact that the mental anguish the Son of God went through was so intense, He began to sweat blood. When is the last time you were so stressed or mentally oppressed that you sweated blood? I didn't think so! But Jesus did. What was the fight about? It was about the temptation to violate the restraining principle upon His life. The first Adam broke the restraining principle upon his life in the Garden of Eden in order to join his bride (Eve) in her sin. Adam *chose his will over God's will.* God's will had already been declared earlier on: "thou shall not eat from the tree of the knowledge of good and evil!"

They say history has a way of repeating itself. Over 4,000 years later the Last Adam (Jesus) was also in a garden, wrestling with the same "serpent" over the exact same issue—whether or not the Last Adam (Jesus) would also violate the divine restraining order on His life by choosing His will over that of His Father. Thankfully, the battle ends in glorious triumph with Jesus saying, "*Nevertheless not My will, but Yours, be done.*" The expression, "*and being in agony, He prayed more earnestly*" implies that praying more earnestly is one of the ways we can increase the grace to stay true to the restraining principle upon our lives. This fact is corroborated by the following statement: "*When He rose up from prayer, and had come to His disciples, He found them sleeping from sorrow.*" Notice how He rose up from prayer but His disciples were found sleeping in the sorrowfulness a prayer-less life brings. *Come on! Get yourself together!* Start praying really hard and watch God empower you to stay true to the restraining principle on your life!

Life Application
S E C T I O N

Memory Verse

Then Jesus answered and said to them, "Most assuredly, I say to you, the Son can do nothing of Himself, but what He sees the Father do; for whatever He does, the Son also does in like manner" (John 5:19).

Reflections

1. What is the principle of divine restraint?

2. Why did Samson lose his supernatural strength?

Chapter 3

Understanding DIVINE
Restraining Orders

*Then the king said to the man of God, "Come home with
me and refresh yourself, and I will give you a reward."
But the man of God said to the king, "If you were to give
me half your house, I would not go in with you; nor would
I eat bread nor drink water in this place. For so it was
commanded me by the word of the Lord, saying, 'You
shall not eat bread, nor drink water, nor return by the
same way you came.'" So he went another way and did
not return by the way he came to Bethel.*

—1 Kings 13:7-10

I N this chapter, I want to help you understand *divine restraining
orders* and how they work. However, I just want to make a couple
of statements about restraining orders in general before I begin
to teach you about *divine* restraining orders. It is very interesting to
me just how much of our present-day judicial system is based on the
heavenly template that God gave to Moses on Mount Sinai. Many

nations, in their global march toward godless secularism, are trying to ignore God altogether in the public square. But they cannot walk away from the justice system that God put together because it's the best judicial system for any law-abiding nation. While secular America is pulling the display of the Ten Commandments from public buildings, including courthouses, the greatest irony is that our entire American judicial system is still following the Mosaic framework of law and order Moses put together. This is due to the simple fact that you cannot run away from God's judicial system without unleashing anarchy in the social fabric of the nation.

Judges and Restraining Orders

You shall appoint judges and officers in all your gates, which the Lord your God gives you, according to your tribes, and they shall judge the people with just judgment (Deuteronomy 16:18).

First of all, let me make this very important statement. *A judge in a court of law is the only person who can impose a restraining or protective order over an entity or individual.* This means that restraining orders fall under the judicial branch of government. How many of God's children realize that the Kingdom of God is actually a self-sustaining and sovereign government? It is a very real government with a country (heaven) and citizenry. Without a doubt, there is no spiritual or earthly government that can survive without a proper judicial system. This is why Robert Henderson's revelation on *Operating in the Courts of Heaven* is extremely important for the betterment of the global Body of Christ. I believe that God is using men like Robert

Henderson to introduce the church to the judicial side of the government of God. Let's be honest, the Body of Christ for the most part has not been aware of God's burning passion for justice. I believe this is also why even the "grace message" is not being applied properly because it is being applied as though grace excuses God from being the Judge of the whole earth. I believe in the "grace message" to the extent that it does not overthrow God's own judicial system that His Kingdom is founded upon.

The Throne of Grace and the Courts of Heaven

> *For we do not have a High Priest who cannot sympathize with our weaknesses, but was in all points tempted as we are, yet without sin. Let us therefore come boldly to the throne of grace, that we may obtain mercy and find grace to help in time of need* (Hebrews 4:15-16).

Without a doubt, every government has several courts within the judicial branch of government. In most law-abiding nations, there are many courts such as lower courts, district courts, magistrate courts, probate courts, high courts, appellate courts, and supreme courts. This being the case, there are also many courts in heaven within God's judicial system. One of those courts is the "Throne of Grace." Perhaps this is the most well-known court of heaven by most followers of Christ. This is the court where we appear when we are overcome with personal sin and weaknesses. We are admonished by the writer of Hebrews to approach this court with boldness knowing that we will obtain mercy and find grace to help us in our time of need.

However, the "Throne of Grace" is not the only court among the Courts of Heaven. But you wouldn't know that if you listened to the teachings of many grace-message teachers. Somehow, some of the proponents of the grace message are teaching the grace message as if the grace of God releases the Kingdom of God from the judicial side of God's everlasting government. Nothing could be further from the truth. This explains why much of the grace message that is being taught today makes people act as though there are no divine or spiritual repercussions to living as they please.

This is a gross miscalculation and misapplication of the grace of God. When you have a judicial system in any country, it is considered an insult to the integrity of the nation's judicial system to simply ignore blatant violations of law. How are you going to trust the American justice system if you find that the justice system is not being applied equitably? The entire judicial system of any country is under the threat of civil disobedience or collapsing when citizens begin to feel as though the justice system is not applied equitably. The Lord knows that this is true of any judicial system, including His. This principle of fairness is the reason God has no partiality in the application of justice. God has no favoritism because the judicial side of His Kingdom does not allow Him to show partiality. Even under this beautiful dispensation of grace, God never abolished heaven's eternal judicial systems. That said, the grace of God is the reason we can easily access the Courts of Heaven. In this chapter, as we talk about divine restraining orders, we will be coming from the judicial side of the government of God.

Defining Restraining Orders

Below is a legal definition of a restraining order or what is also known as a protective order in most earthly judicial systems. A restraining order or a protective order is designed to protect something. A simple legal definition of "restraining orders" as per the world we live in is as follows:

> A restraining order or protective order is an order issued by a court to protect a person, business, company, establishment, or entity, and the general public, in a situation involving alleged domestic violence, assault, harassment, stalking, or sexual assault.[1]

The above definition is the legal and widely accepted definition of a restraining order in this natural dimension we call the world. This definition, for the most part, is intercontinental. The legal definition of a restraining order also clearly establishes why they are also known as protective orders. They are clearly awarded by the courts to protect a person or an entity from suffering irreparable damage in emergency situations. However, it is neither the intention nor purpose of this book to discuss the application of natural restraining orders. We only discuss the definition and importance of natural restraining orders in order to paint a clear picture why ambassadors of Christ must understand the importance of divine restraining orders and how to apply them.

Defining Divine Restraining Orders

For behold, you shall conceive and bear a son. And no razor shall come upon his head, for the child shall be a Nazirite to God from the womb; and he shall begin to deliver Israel out of the hand of the Philistines (Judges 13:5).

At this juncture, I want to delve into divine restraining orders. We are going to look at a couple of scriptures to help us understand divine restraining orders. When the Lord began to teach me about divine restraining orders, I was the guinea pig He used to demonstrate the importance of obeying divine restraining orders. I remember when I was living in South Africa in the '90s; I was functioning as a healing evangelist during that time. I borrowed a car from a white woman who was part of my evangelistic ministry. I was preaching in a crusade in a predominantly black township known as Mamelodi. One night after a very powerful night of miracles, signs, and wonders, I drove home gleefully. I was on cloud nine! The song "Jesus Is Alive" by Ron Kenoly was playing in the background. Nothing could go wrong, I thought! When I approached the traffic light I heard a still small voice say to me, "When you get to the traffic light, turn right and use the back route to get to your house." I knew the route the Holy Spirit was suggesting but it meant there'd be extra 20 minutes of driving. I was tired and so I ignored the warning.

When I stopped at the second traffic light, a truck driver hit me from behind. My little Toyota Corolla was severely damaged. After the accident, my heart was pounding profusely because I knew the car was borrowed. Then I heard the same still small voice say to me, "All you had to do to avoid the accident was turn right at the traffic light like I told you." I had no idea at the time that the Lord had applied a divine restraining order from the Courts of Heaven when He told me to turn right at the first traffic light. My judgment for violating a divine restraining order was immediate.

When the police finally arrived, I discovered to my utter dismay that the truck driver did not have car insurance. He was what South Africans called "night drivers." These were drivers who had no driver's license or insurance so they drove at night in hopes of avoiding the police. This meant I was responsible for fixing my friend's damaged car. It cost me six months of my honorariums to finally fix my friend's car. Throughout this whole time, the Holy Spirit told me sternly, "Do not make the mistake of going left when I tell you to go to right." Trust me, I got the message!

This leads me to the million-dollar question: "What is a divine restraining order?"

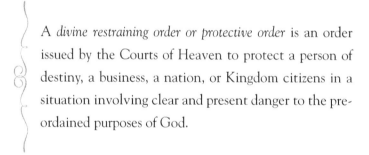

A *divine restraining order or protective order* is an order issued by the Courts of Heaven to protect a person of destiny, a business, a nation, or Kingdom citizens in a situation involving clear and present danger to the pre-ordained purposes of God.

Sometimes divine restraining orders are also put in place by the Courts of Heaven to give a child of God time to get their act together. We are going to go deeper into this aspect of divine restraining orders. One of the main problems that is giving the accuser of the brethren legal standing to resist the destinies of so many of God's children is that many of them, like Samson, are guilty of violating the divine restraining orders that God imposed upon their lives. These violations of divine restraining orders must first be repented of before some of God's children can experience total breakthrough. Once the Lord said to me, *"There have been a lot of violations of divine restraining orders in the Body of Christ and there are legal cases that have piled up against them in the Courts of Heaven."* In a later chapter, I am going to deal with what happens when a person violates a divine restraining order. The last chapter of this book is stockpiled with prayers of activation to help you approach the Courts of Heaven and request the application of a divine restraining order over your life against demonic powers and destiny killers.

Life Application
S E C T I O N

Memory Verse

"For so it was commanded me by the word of the Lord, saying, 'You shall not eat bread, nor drink water, nor return by the same way you came.'" So he went another way and did not return by the way he came to Bethel (1 Kings 13:9-10).

Reflections

1. What is a divine restraining order?

2. Have you ever violated a divine restraining order?

Chapter 4

The Lifestyle *of an* Officer *of the*
COURTS *of* HEAVEN

And I said, "Let them put a clean turban on his head."
So they put a clean turban on his head, and they put the
clothes on him. And the Angel of the Lord stood by. Then
the Angel of the Lord admonished Joshua, saying, "Thus
says the Lord of hosts: 'If you will walk in My ways, and
if you will keep My command, then you shall also judge
My house, and likewise have charge of My courts; I will
give you places to walk among these who stand here.'"

—Zechariah 3:5-7

BEFORE we go deeper into understanding and applying
divine restraining orders, I believe the Lord wants me to talk
about the *lifestyle of an officer of the Courts of Heaven*. When
Apostle Robert Henderson was preaching at our church (Lovefest-
church.com), I was very blessed when in one of his messages he dealt

with the importance of *lifestyle* for people who want to become skilled at operating in the Courts of Heaven. Robert made this statement: "The more you die to self, the more power God will grant you before the Courts of Heaven." I agreed with him completely, and I will elaborate further in this chapter.

Growing in Stature with God and Man!

> *And Jesus increased in wisdom and stature, and in favor with God and men* (Luke 2:52).

You see, there is such a thing as *stature* in the spiritual realm, which is totally different from the anointing of God upon your charisma or gift. Spiritual stature is a very real and tradable currency in the spirit world. Whereas the anointing is divine empowerment by the Holy Spirit, *stature is galvanized from the life you provide to God as a living sacrifice by constantly yielding your will, mind, and emotions to the leading of His Spirit.* This is the critical difference between the anointing and stature. Stature is what we need the most in order to operate effectively in the Courts of Heaven. The Bible tells us that Jesus grew in stature, not just in the anointing. As a matter of fact, Jesus grew in stature before the anointing of the Holy Spirit fell on Him after John the Baptist baptized Him in the Jordan River (see Matt. 3).

The real problem in the Body of Christ is that we have lots of people who are anointed but they don't have spiritual stature with God and man. According to Luke 2:52, when we grow in spiritual stature we gain favor with God and man. This is because *stature* has to do with *legal standing*. Favor with God means that God gives us the grace to summon His presence and judicial power to rule on our behalf. Favor with man means that God allows people to be naturally drawn to us and find us believable when we speak or pray on God's behalf. *I don't know about you, but I desperately want to grow in stature and favor with God and man.* I have too much on my plate to do for God's Kingdom to waste my time trying to convince both God and man to move on my behalf.

> *Then the disciples came to Jesus privately and said, "Why could we not cast it out?" So Jesus said to them, "Because of your unbelief; for assuredly, I say to you, if you have faith as a mustard seed, you will say to this mountain, 'Move from here to there,' and it will move; and nothing will be impossible for you"* (Matthew 17:19-20).

Have you ever wondered why some people can pray and things open up in the spirit world immediately but when you pray nothing happens? This is due to the fact that they have cultivated their spiritual stature and have a lifestyle to prove it and you don't. Without a doubt, we are all children of God, but we don't live for the Lord in the same manner. Even though we are all children of God, not every child of God walks in the fear of the Lord. Some Christians treat God as though He is one of their distant cousins. They act like what He tells them to do is a nice suggestion instead of a royal command. Then there are those who are willing to lay down their lives to obey the Lord. Consequently, they have stature with God because of the way they live.

The Lifestyle of an Officer of the Court

The Lord told me there is a lifestyle that is required before people can be trusted with becoming officers of the Courts of Heaven, who can actually apply divine restraining orders. The Lord said to me, "Applying divine restraining orders is one aspect of the Courts of Heaven that cannot be applied by every child of God." This does not mean children of God cannot approach the Courts of Heaven to request a divine restraining order against a person or situation that poses immediate danger to their well-being. The last chapter of this book will deal with activation prayers for requesting divine restraining orders. This is the good news—every blood-washed child of God can approach the Courts and request restraining orders under the right conditions.

However, applying or imposing divine restraining orders (like natural restraining orders) is the function of a judge in any judicial system. This means only the Righteous Judge, certain high-ranking angels, and human officers of the Courts of Heaven who have moved from plaintiff to judge can impose divine restraining orders in the earth realm. In the next chapter, I will teach you how to move from plaintiff to judge in the Courts of Heaven. As I go deeper into the lifestyle of an officer of the Courts of Heaven, you will begin to understand why this is so important to the whole subject of *operating in the Courts of Heaven*. God has to trust you with the *power* to impose divine restraining orders. This is why you have to cultivate your spiritual stature in the Courts of Heaven. We will now examine Zechariah 3:5-7 and Revelation 12:11 to fully appreciate the lifestyle of an officer of the Courts of Heaven.

1. Putting on the Mind of Christ

And I said, "Let them put a clean turban on his head." So they put a clean turban on his head, and they put the clothes on him. And the Angel of the Lord stood by (Zechariah 3:5).

There is no mind that is healthier than the mind of Christ. Jesus Christ had the healthiest mind of any human being who has ever lived. The mind of Christ was healthier than the mind of the first Adam. Even though Adam's mind was a genius mind (he could use his mind to remember the names of all the animals on planet Earth), his mind could never compete with the mind of Christ. Jesus had such a healthy mind that even though every form of temptation imaginable surrounded Him, He never sinned with His mind—not once. I definitely cannot say that about myself. Only God knows how many times I have sinned with my mind only to repent later. I'm sure I'm not on an island here all by myself.

The expression in the book of Zechariah, *"Let them put a clean turban on his head,"* is a prophetic picture of putting on the mind of Christ. We are admonished by the Word of God to put on the mind of Christ. In order to put on the mind of Christ, we must divorce ourselves from the old mind that belonged to the old carnal nature with its unending sinful desires. This means that you cannot be an officer of the Courts of Heaven with a dirty mind. The good news is that the blood of Jesus is more than able to wash our minds clean. When the Angel of the Lord (Jesus) instructed the holy angels in the Courts of Heaven to *put a clean turban on Joshua's head*, the Lord effectively sanctified his mind. Are you willing to allow the Lord to sanctify your mind so you can become an effective officer of the Courts of Heaven?

2. Clothed in Righteousness

And I said, "Let them put a clean turban on his head." So they put a clean turban on his head, and they put the clothes on him. And the Angel of the Lord stood by (Zechariah 3:5).

The Angel of the Lord makes another important request. He instructs angelic officers of the courts to clothe Joshua in rich, clean, and royal robes of righteousness. In prophetic language, "clothes" always represent either righteousness or sin. If the clothes are clean, it means someone is clothed in righteousness. On the other hand, if the clothes are dirty, it means that a person is clothed in sin or iniquity. God is a God of righteousness, so He won't allow human officers of the Courts of Heaven to come before Him clothed in the sin nature or harboring unconfessed personal sin. Most importantly, *righteousness* is not a religious term. It's a legal term that law students learn in law school, and it means "right standing with a governing authority or judge."

Righteousness in a biblical sense simply means "to be in right standing with God or with a governing authority." This also implies that when a person is a fugitive from the law, he or she is not in right standing with the government and its justice department.

This is what Adam's sin in the Garden of Eden did to all of mankind. It made us spiritual fugitives from the law of God until Jesus paid the price for us to be righteous again. This is why righteousness is the most important condition of an officer of any judicial system, especially the Courts of Heaven. Joshua could never become an officer of the Courts of Heaven until he was fully clothed or robed in righteousness. Are you clothed in righteousness? If you're not, the Bible says,

"If we confess our sins, He is faithful and just to forgive us our sins and to cleanse us from all unrighteousness" (1 John 1:9).

3. Walking in the Ways of the Spirit

> *Then the Angel of the Lord admonished Joshua, saying, "Thus says the Lord of hosts: 'If you will walk in My ways…'"* (Zechariah 3:6-7).

The Angel of the Lord further admonishes Joshua and says, *"If you will walk in My ways."* This expression "walking in my ways" is extremely important for us to understand. It goes without saying that the ways of the Lord are not our ways. "Ways of the Lord" are ancient paths, blueprints, systems, behaviors, and methodologies that God uses, at His discretion, to do the counsel of His will. For instance, God chose to heal Naaman's leprosy in the dirty Jordan River instead of using the sensational, sky-blue waters of the Damascus River. Naaman almost lost his chance at a miracle because he felt humiliated by the *way* God chose to heal him (see 2 Kings 5).

One of my favorite biblical passages concerning the ways of the Lord is directly related to Moses and Israel. *"He made known His ways to Moses, His acts to the children of Israel"* (Ps. 103:7). This scripture means that Moses, the man of God, had a revelation of the "ways of the Spirit" while the rest of Israel only knew what God did (acts) and not why He did it (ways). It's obvious to me that the Angel of the Lord wanted Joshua to know that if he was going to be an effective officer of the Courts of Heaven, he had to be completely dependent on the leading of the Holy Spirit. When Brother Robert Henderson was leading our congregation into the Courts of Heaven, I was quite impressed to see how much he relies on the leading of the Holy Spirit each time he does it. Unfortunately, there are copycats in the diaspora who lead people into the Courts of Heaven mechanically without the leading of the Holy Spirit. This is why the people who are following them are not experiencing real spiritual breakthroughs.

Operating in the Courts of Heaven will require a high level of dependency on the leading of the Holy Spirit. The Holy Spirit is the most important officer of the Courts of Heaven because without Him we would have zero access to the spirit world. Even though we can request an appearance before the Courts of Heaven through the blood of Jesus, it's the Holy Spirit who manifests the reality of the Courts of Heaven. The Courts of Heaven do not manifest or operate outside of the guiding influence of the third member of the Godhead. Jesus even said so: *"And when He has come, He will convict the world of sin, and of righteousness, and of judgment"* (John 16:8). Notice that the words Jesus uses here—*convict, sin, righteousness,* and *judgment*—all relate to the Courts of Heaven. *Only a court of law can convict, acquit, or pass judgment on anybody,* and Jesus is showing us in this passage that the Holy Spirit is, without doubt, the most important officer of the Courts of Heaven here on earth. So it goes without saying that to become an effective officer of the Courts of Heaven we must be completely submitted to the leading of the Holy Spirit.

4. The Covenant of Total Obedience

> *Thus says the Lord of hosts: "If you will walk in My ways, and if you will keep My command, then you shall also judge My house, and likewise have charge of My courts; I will give you places to walk among these who stand here"* (Zechariah 3:7).

The expression in the book of Zechariah, *"and if you will keep My command, then you shall also judge My house,"* is a direct reference to the importance of obedience to God in the life of a human officer of the Courts of Heaven. There is nothing more important to God than the covenant of total obedience. Why? It is the covenant of total obedience that placed Jesus on the cross. Remove obedience to God in the heart of Jesus and He would never have died such a horrible death on the cross to atone for our sin. The principle of obedience in the heart of Jesus came into full view in the famous agony of our Savior in the Garden of Gethsemane. In the Garden of Gethsemane, the Lord Jesus Christ fought his greatest battle yet. *It was a spiritual battle between the will of God and the will of the Son of Man.* It was the same spiritual battle that took place between Adam's will and the will of God in the Garden of Eden. The first Adam chose his will, while the last Adam (Jesus) chose God's perfect will. The battle was so intense that Jesus began to sweat blood. Thankfully, the battle ended beautifully with Jesus saying, *"Father, if it is Your will, take this cup away from Me; nevertheless not My will, but Yours, be done"* (Luke 22:42).

Operating in the Courts of Heaven will require us to be obedient to both the voice of the Lord and the protocol of the Courts of Heaven. We cannot present legal cases before the Courts of Heaven in a spirit of disobedience. Disobedience is a byproduct of the kingdom of darkness. Walking in disobedience brings us under Satan's dominion. If we are living in disobedience, we compromise our legal standing and jurisdiction before the Courts of Heaven. Satan, our number-one nemesis and accuser of the brethren, is going to use our disobedience to God as a legal threshold to resist our petition before the Courts of Heaven. When Apostle Robert Henderson was teaching on the Courts of Heaven in our church, he said, *"You can never do enough repenting when it comes to operating in the Courts of Heaven. This is because repenting before the Lord for known and unknown sins before we proceed to present our legal case before the Lord can never hurt us, even if we overdo it."* Repentance for a child of God is like having the Holy Communion. You can never do it enough, and doing it more than once does not hurt us, spiritually speaking. That said, God requires a spirit of obedience in the hearts of human officers of the Courts of Heaven.

5. Laying Your Life Down as a Living Sacrifice

And they overcame him by the blood of the Lamb and by the word of their testimony, and they did not love their lives to the death (Revelation 12:11).

There is no greater offering we can give to the Lord than our very life. Giving money to the church while refusing to surrender our lives to the Lord won't do us too much good in the long run. The testimony of Scripture is quite clear. God would rather have your life than your earthly possessions. Think about this—how can a God who owns everything in creation be impressed with you when you give Him a car, money, or a house? God already owned the stuff before you gave it to Him. What He does not automatically own, even though He is Lord of all, is *your free will.* Man's free will is what makes him exactly like God. As human beings, we can choose to love or hate, obey or disobey. This is why the expression "*and they did not love their lives to the death*" in Revelation 12:11 is a very explosive statement. It means the persons in question chose with their own free will "not to love their own lives" to the point of martyrdom. This is the greatest offering a human can ever give to a God who alone knows the priceless nature of "free will."

When Robert Henderson was teaching on the Courts of Heaven at our church, he made this statement: "When we lay down our life as a living sacrifice, we get more power in the Courts of Heaven." As a man who grew up in Africa, I truly understand the importance of altars. I know firsthand the power of altars. All the witchcraft that has terrorized Africa is connected to altars our forefathers dedicated to demon gods.

However, the story of altars as places of sacrifice and worship is rooted in the teaching of Scripture. God is a God who loves to visit people at altars. In the Old Testament, whenever Abraham, Isaac, Jacob, Moses, or King David built an altar, God's glory was visited upon the entire nation speedily. Why? This is because altars represent man laying down his life willingly as a living sacrifice before the Lord. If you and I want to become effective officers of the Courts of Heaven, we need to lay down our lives as a living sacrifice before the Lord (see Rom. 12:1-2).

6. Walking in Humility

The final but not the least of all: God wants us to walk in humility. There are fewer things God treasures more than humility. The fall of Lucifer is due to an intersection between pride and rebellion. Pride corrupted Lucifer's wisdom by reason of his immense beauty. Instead of trading in humility, he introduced a wrong trading platform in the Courts of Heaven—pride. *"Your heart was lifted up because of your beauty; you corrupted your wisdom for the sake of your splendor* (Ezek. 28:17). Since then, Satan or Leviathan, is the lord of the "children of pride." *"He beholds every high thing; he is king over all the children of pride"* (Job 41:34). We must remember that the more God uses us in the Courts of Heaven, the more humility we will need to walk in.

Humility robs the accuser of any legal footing to resist our judicial authority and standing before the Courts of Heaven. Most importantly, the Bible is very clear that God resists the proud and gives grace to those who are humble (see James 4:6). Walking in pride is the quickest way to lose our legal standing before the Courts of Heaven. This is why the Holy Spirit requires humility in all human and celestial officers of the Courts of Heaven.

Life Application
S E C T I O N

Memory Verse

Thus says the Lord of hosts: "If you will walk in My ways, and if you will keep My command, then you shall also judge My house, and likewise have charge of My courts; I will give you places to walk among these who stand here" (Zechariah 3:7).

Reflections

1. What evidence did Satan have against Joshua, the high priest?

2. Has the Lord shown you anything in your life that the devil is using to accuse you in the Courts of Heaven?

Chapter 5

Transitioning
from PLAINTIFF
to JUDGE

But you have come to Mount Zion and to the city of the living God, the heavenly Jerusalem, to an innumerable company of angels, to the general assembly and church of the firstborn who are registered in heaven, to God the Judge of all, to the spirits of just men made perfect, to Jesus the Mediator of the new covenant, and to the blood of sprinkling that speaks better things than that of Abel.

— Hebrews 12:22-24

DUE to the shed blood of Christ that is constantly "speaking and proclaiming its judicial testimony" on our behalf (Heb. 12:24), combined with the finished work of Christ on the cross, we have been given a glorious opportunity to come before the

Courts of Heaven in a spirit of boldness. One of the most important Courts of Heaven is the Throne of Grace. One of the courts is the "court of nations" where the affairs of nations and its rulers are judged (see Dan. 5:1-15). However, I also want you to understand that we have also been given the legal authority to present our cases as plaintiffs before the Courts of Heaven.

> *"Present your case," says the Lord. "Bring forth your strong reasons," says the King of Jacob* (Isaiah 41:21).

When the accuser brings an accusation against us in the Courts of Heaven, he is merely giving us the opportunity to ask Jesus, our loyal Advocate in the Courts of Heaven, to represent us before the Righteous Judge.

> *My little children, these things I write to you, so that you may not sin. And if anyone sins, we have an Advocate with the Father, Jesus Christ the righteous* (1 John 2:1).

I must address a very important aspect of the Courts of Heaven here. Whereas it is exciting for us to present our cases before the Courts of Heaven as plaintiffs, it is important to recognize that the stature of a plaintiff in any courtroom is much lower than that of other officers of the court. For instance, a bailiff, arresting officer, advocate, prosecutor, and court clerk have a higher ranking in the courtroom than a plaintiff. Obviously, both the stature and legal standing of a judge in a courtroom is much higher than that of any other officer of the court. When the Lord showed me this He said to me, *"I want to change the position of many of My people from plaintiff to judge in My Courts, if they are willing to provide Me with the lifestyle I require for this transition."*

The Great Transition

The Lord took me to the book of Zechariah to show me how any child of God can transition from plaintiff to judge within the Courts of Heaven. I was wonderfully surprised when I saw it! In Zechariah 3, God gives us a glimpse into a heavenly courtroom trial in progress. We will analyze this amazing courtroom drama to see how the Lord Jesus (Angel of the Lord) took Joshua the High Priest from plaintiff to a judge in the Courts of God. We will see how God changes the spiritual stature of a child of God from plaintiff to judge. God literally walks Joshua through the whole process of becoming a judge within the Courts of Heaven. Are you aware that you have not just been called to be a plaintiff in the Courts of Heaven? God wants to grow you up to become judge in the spirit world. Samuel was more than a prophet in Israel. He was a judge. He was a human representative here on earth on behalf of the Courts of Heaven. This is why Samuel's judgments were binding in both heaven and earth.

Check this out! If Samuel, an Old Testament saint, was a judge in the Courts of Heaven, why can't you also be a judge under the New Covenant? I believe, my friend Apostle Robert Henderson is one of the judges on behalf of the Courts of Heaven whom God has raised in our generation. God is using him, and others like him, to execute God's righteous judgments on behalf of people whose destinies have been stalled by the accuser of the brethren. When Robert took my wife and me through the Courts of Heaven to present our case, there was an immediate breakthrough in our lives. The judgment of God against what was holding us back came speedily because we had gone before the Courts of Heaven with a man who was actually a judge in the spirit and not just a plaintiff. I believe God wants to raise many judges in the Body of Christ who have the lifestyle of an officer of the Courts of Heaven.

God cannot trust many people in the Body of Christ with judgment over His own house. This is due to the fact that many so-called born-again Christians are not dead enough to the flesh to become judges in the spirit. Did you know that one of the things that judges are not allowed to do is bring their own emotions or biases into a case over which they are presiding? When a judge brings his or her emotional biases into any case, they open themselves up to an appeal. This is why judges in higher courts can overrule another judge's sentence when they find that the judge's emotional involvement with a case created a material conflict of interest or impelled the rule of law.

When you are a judge, you are supposed to be impartial; even if you like the plaintiff, you cannot show favoritism as a judge. Why? This is due to the fact that you have a stature in the courtroom; all legal proceedings within the courtroom rely on the judge's impartiality in order to uphold the rule of law. This is why Robert Henderson's book *Operating in the Courts of Heaven* is very important to the Body of Christ. If you have not read Robert's book that I am referencing, I advise that you get it immediately. Robert's book will teach you the protocols of operating in the Courts of Heaven. God is a Righteous Judge who cannot show favoritism that violates the rule of law just to deliver His children. Instead, our heavenly Father wants to teach us how to approach His judicial bench, accurately. This way, we can give Him the legal right He is looking for to do for us what He longs to do on our behalf as our loving heavenly Father.

Joshua's Journey: From Plaintiff to Judge

Let's see how God moved Joshua from a plaintiff to a judge in the courts of our God. Let us look at Zechariah 3, verse by verse:

*Then he showed me Joshua the high priest standing before
the Angel of the Lord, and Satan standing at his right hand
to oppose him* (Zechariah 3:1).

The heavenly courtroom drama opens up with Joshua, the high
priest, standing before the Angel of the Lord. Bible scholars agree
that the title "Angel of the Lord" is one of the Old Testament titles
of Yeshua (the Messiah). Melchizedek is another reference to Jesus,
but that is a subject for another book. In this heavenly courtroom
trial of Joshua, the Angel of the Lord is the Advocate in this case. He
is in the courtroom as Joshua's defense attorney. On the other hand,
Satan is present in the courtroom as the "accuser or prosecutor." The
word *Satan* simply means "accuser." However, Satan is not an accuser
in the same sense as a village drunk who brings up a railing accusation against someone because he has had too much booze. Many
Christians think this way about Satan; they are failing to materialize
their God-given destinies because they fail to recognize that Satan
has actual legal standing for his accusations. Satan accuses us *day and
night* before God in the face of irrefutable evidence. Otherwise, God
would throw him out of the Courts of Heaven. There is no self-respecting judge or court who will hear a case where the prosecutor has
failed to prove standing for a case on which they want the court to
adjudicate. God, the Righteous Judge, is no different.

What I love about this story is that it is a heavenly courtroom
drama that actually happened. It was not a parable or allegory that
was told to stimulate our imagination or merely to entertain us. As
this courtroom drama plays out, the Holy Spirit wants us to understand how this ordinary man, Joshua, moves from plaintiff to judge
within heaven's judicial system. Isn't it amazing to begin as a plaintiff
and end up becoming a judge before the case is over?

Satan was positioned on Joshua's right-hand side to oppose him before the Courts of Heaven due to evidence he had gathered against him. Robert Henderson believes that some of the evidence that Satan had gathered against Joshua came from visiting his generational bloodline. Satan definitely had a legal case to present before the Lord. Otherwise, he wouldn't have had "standing" before the Courts of Heaven. Do you know that the Supreme Court of the United States of America (SCOTUS) never hears many of the cases that are presented to it? Why? This is due to the fact that SCOTUS imposes a legitimate legal test before a case can come before the Supreme Court of the United States.

The main litmus test is the issue called "standing." The nine justices use this litmus test to decide which cases can be heard or rejected. A lot of cases are rejected because they do not have "standing or precedence" to go before the highest court in the land. So, if Satan is before the highest court in the universe, the Supreme Court of Heaven, he must have had legal "standing." And the fact that the Lord Jesus (Angel of the Lord) is also present in the courtroom as an advocate on Joshua's behalf means that the devil had already proven the issue of "standing" before Joshua was put on trial. Since Satan (the prosecutor) and the Advocate (the Angel of the Lord) are both in the courtroom, they both agreed on one thing: Satan had gathered enough evidence to put Joshua on trial in the Courts of Heaven.

Two Redeeming Principles

And the Lord said to Satan, "The Lord rebuke you, Satan! The Lord who has chosen Jerusalem rebuke you! Is this not a brand plucked from the fire?" (Zechariah 3:2)

Joshua's trial starts out with the Lord rebuking Satan in the name of the Lord on the basis that God had chosen Jerusalem as the city of the living God! Then the Angel of the Lord further rebukes Satan's accusatory position in the Courts of Heaven by asking the court this question: *"Is this [Joshua] not the brand plucked from the fire?"* The opening statement by the Angel of the Lord sets in place two redeeming principles that the Lord uses to begin to lay ground for a righteous verdict on our behalf:

1. The first redeeming principle the Lord Jesus (our Advocate) uses in the Courts of Heaven to issue righteous verdicts on our behalf has do with God's commitment to His own predetermined purposes. The expression, *"The Lord who has chosen Jerusalem rebuke you"* suggests that the main appeal for Joshua's acquittal before the Courts of Heaven was because God had chosen Jerusalem as part of His eternal purposes. God's eternal counsel always stands the test of time, so it's a pretty huge appeal for the acquittal of a man (Joshua) who was intricately connected to the manifestation of that purpose. *"Declaring the end from the beginning, and from ancient times things that are not yet done, saying, 'My counsel shall stand, and I will do all My pleasure'"* (Isa. 46:10). The Angel of the Lord appeals to the Righteous Judge to consider Joshua's role as high priest over Jerusalem as part of the mitigating evidence for his acquittal.

2. The second redeeming principle the Lord Jesus (our Advocate) uses in the Courts of Heaven to issue righteous verdicts on our behalf has do with the fact that He is our kinsman redeemer. The Angel of the Lord appeals to the court to consider the fact that Joshua was a brand plucked from the fire of sin by the mercy of the Lord. *"For judgment is without mercy to the one who has shown no mercy. Mercy*

triumphs over judgment" (James 2:13). The mercy of the Lord toward sinners is one of the main reasons we always have a shot at an acquittal in the Courts of Heaven. Most especially under the New Covenant because Jesus' shed blood and Christ's finished work on the cross are also considered as mitigating evidence for our acquittal.

Satan's Evidence

We will now quickly look through Satan's evidence that he brought before the Courts of Heaven against Joshua the high priest. It is important for us to understand Satan's evidence because it's what he uses regularly to resist the fulfillment of our destinies in the earth realm.

1. Joshua was clothed with filthy garments.

Now Joshua was clothed with filthy garments, and was standing before the Angel. Then He answered and spoke to those who stood before Him, saying, "Take away the filthy garments from him" (Zechariah 3:3-4).

The first piece of evidence Satan had gathered against Joshua was the fact that "*Joshua was clothed with filthy garments.*" Filthy garments in Scripture always represent sin or man's self-righteousness. "*But we are all like an unclean thing, and all our righteousness are like filthy rags; we all fade as a leaf, and our iniquities, like the wind, have taken us away*" (Isa. 64:6). Joshua's filthy garments had given the devil *sufficient legal grounds* for God the Righteous Judge to grant him a court date. Even though God wanted Joshua to serve as high priest over Jerusalem, the Lord could not ignore the mountain of evidence Satan had gathered against him. Thankfully, Jesus' death and shed blood is the basis for cleansing us from the filthy garments of our sin. When the Angel of the Lord instructed angelic officers of the court to "take away Joshua's filthy garments," He was essentially taking away the legal standing the enemy had against him. The expression "I'll clothe you with rich robes" is a divine promise that God can always clothe us in righteousness if we come to Him in heartfelt repentance.

2. "See, I have removed your iniquity from you."

And to him He said, "See, I have removed your iniquity from you, and I will clothe you with rich robes" (Zechariah 3:4).

The second piece of evidence Satan had gathered against Joshua was based upon the "iniquity" in his ancestral bloodline. "Iniquity" is about hidden sin. For the most part, it deals with sinful actions of past generations of ancestors. Apparently, there was enough iniquity attached to Joshua's bloodline to give Satan the legal standing he needed to bring a lawsuit against him before the Courts of Heaven. An iniquity is also a "lawless act or transgression of God's law." This means that every action that violates God's law that is perpetuated by members of any bloodline creates an iniquity against that particular bloodline. If iniquities are actions against God's law in any generational bloodline, the longer a person's lineage, the greater the number of iniquities attached to that particular bloodline.

It's wisdom at this point to define the word *lineage* in the context of the subject of iniquities. A "lineage" is a sequence of species that form a line of descent. Each new species in the lineage is the direct result of speciation from an immediate ancestral species.

Generational curses are based upon iniquities that have taken place in a particular ancestral bloodline, so Satan has every legal right to use them as footholds for resisting our destinies from coming forth. This is exactly what he was doing against Joshua in the Courts of Heaven.

3. "Let them put a clean turban on his head."

And I said, "Let them put a clean turban on his head." So they put a clean turban on his head, and they put the clothes on him. And the Angel of the Lord stood by (Zechariah 3:5).

The third piece of evidence Satan had gathered against Joshua was implied in the Lord's instruction to His angelic officers of the Courts of Heaven. He said, *"Let them put a clean turban on his head."* The clean turban on Joshua's head represents a clean and healthy mind. This means that part of Satan's legal standing had to do with the spiritual condition of Joshua's mind. Satan had probably found impure thoughts in Joshua's mind. He had discovered thinking patterns or mindsets in Joshua's mind that were more aligned with the kingdom of darkness than with the Kingdom of God. The writer of Proverbs tells us this: *"For as he thinks in his heart, so is he"* (Prov. 23:7)! Sometimes, how we think can give the devil a legal footing to resist our God-given destiny or supplant our spiritual authority. Think about this—if we mentally agree with the spirit of poverty, how can God deliver us from it? If we think and believe that we are poor, why would the devil allow money to find its way into our pockets? When the Angel of the Lord instructed that a clean turban be placed upon Joshua's head, He was removing whatever mindset or pattern of thinking that was giving the devil a legal footing.

4. "If you will walk in My ways, and if you will keep My command."

Then the Angel of the Lord admonished Joshua, saying, "Thus says the Lord of hosts: 'If you will walk in My ways, and if you will keep My command...'" (Zechariah 3:6-7).

The fourth piece of evidence Satan had gathered against Joshua was also implied by the Angel of the Lord when He said, *"Thus says the Lord of hosts: 'If you will walk in My ways, and if you will keep My command.'"* This expression means that Satan had irrefutable evidence that Joshua was not:

a. Walking in the ways of the Lord

Satan had evidence that instead of following the leading of the Holy Spirit, Joshua, like many Christians I know, was making things up as he went along. Satan knows that God does not anoint our agenda. He anoints and blesses His perfect will. So many of God's children are mass-producing Ishmaels because they refuse to wait on God's perfect timing. In most cases, it's because they do not know the "ways of the Spirit."

"For My thoughts are not your thoughts, nor are your ways My ways," says the Lord. "For as the heavens are higher than the earth, so are My ways higher than your ways, and My thoughts than your thoughts" (Isaiah 55:8-9).

Obviously, Satan had discovered that Joshua's ways were quite misaligned with the ways of the Lord. How do you measure up against this kind of accusation?

b. Keeping the commandments of the Lord

Satan also had evidence that instead of following the commandments of the Lord, Joshua was doing his own thing. How many Christians talk the "Word" but do not live a life according to the Word of God? Many of God's people are giving Satan too much legal footing against them because they are not obedient to the Word. Disobedience to the Word of God is not going to give us favor or moral authority when we stand before the Righteous Judge. Even the devil knows enough of the Word to know that God has placed His Word above His name (see Ps. 138:2). Living in the Word will increase our spiritual stature and legal standing before the Courts of Heaven. It is my heartfelt prayer that as you read this book the Lord will infuse your spirit with the grace for total obedience.

Becoming a Judge in the Courts of Heaven

> Then the Angel of the Lord admonished Joshua, saying, "Thus says the Lord of hosts: 'If you will walk in My ways, and if you will keep My command, then you shall also judge My house, and likewise have charge of My courts; I will give you places to walk among these who stand here'" (Zechariah 3:6-7).

After the Angel of the Lord dealt with the accuser and demolished his legal standing against Joshua, he revealed something to Joshua that was mind-blowing. I had read this passage of scripture many times and never saw it, until recently! Even though it's clear that it was Satan who had asked for Joshua to be put on trial, the Lord used Satan's lawsuit to radically change Joshua's position in the Courts of

Heaven. When the trial started, Joshua was merely a plaintiff in desperate need of an acquittal. But by the end of his trial, the Angel of the Lord showed him that he had a "higher calling" in the same court.

God wanted Joshua to represent the Courts of Heaven from his heavenly position as judge within the confines of natural Jerusalem. In other words, the Lord was giving Joshua two positions of ministry—one was earthly (high priest) and the other was heavenly (judge in the Courts of Heaven). This transition from plaintiff to judge left me speechless. The Lord wanted Joshua, the high priest, to establish the Courts of Heaven in the temple in Jerusalem. God was calling him to be the high priest over the service of the temple, but He also wanted him to judge Israel. Becoming a judge in the Courts of Heaven was to be Joshua's highest calling. It becomes blatantly obvious why Joshua's trial was a high stakes trial. Satan had somehow caught wind of the fact that the Lord had a higher calling for Joshua in which Satan did not want him to function in. So Satan quickly brought a railing accusation against Joshua's ascension to the high office of judge in the Courts of Heaven.

Check this out! Then the Angel of the Lord admonished Joshua, saying, "*Thus says the Lord of hosts: 'If you will walk in My ways, and if you will keep My command, then you shall also judge My house, and likewise have charge of My courts; I will give you places to walk among these who stand here.'*" Please take note that when Joshua's trial started the Angel of the Lord only addressed Satan and the Righteous Judge, but after Joshua got a righteous verdict of acquittal, the Angel of the Lord completely ignored Satan.

After Joshua's acquittal, the Angel of the Lord began to address Joshua directly. He began to deal with him concerning the whole issue of lifestyle. *The issue of lifestyle was very important because it allowed Joshua to keep his heavenly judicial seat.* This means that if he lost the lifestyle, he would lose his judicial seat in the Courts of Heaven. The

Lord was not going to allow him to judge His people from the standpoint of "flesh" or he would be judging God's people without a direct connection to the Courts of Heaven. When the Angel of the Lord admonished Joshua saying, "*Thus says the Lord of Hosts: 'If you...,'*" "if" in the verse means Joshua had a part to play in the whole process of moving from plaintiff to judge. The word *if* means God will not do anything without our full cooperation. The Angel of the Lord declares, "*If* you walk in My way, *if* you keep My commandments, *then* you shall judge My house!" This statement by the Angel of the Lord implies that if Joshua satisfied the spiritual conditions for his heavenly judicial seat, God would make him a judge over God's house. This means that the Courts of Heaven would support his judgments on earth.

It's Your Time!

Many of you who are reading this book or Robert Henderson's books on the Courts of Heaven have been coming before the Courts of Heaven as plaintiffs, but that time is over! It is time for you to become a judge in the Lord's house. God wants to use you to take other Kingdom citizens before the Courts of Heaven. He wants you to become skilled at the art of executing in the earth realm the righteous judgments of the Lord. God wants to use you to start *issuing divine restraining orders from the Courts of Heaven*. God wants to use you as one of His righteous judges to protect people who are under serious demonic attack by issuing divine restraining orders against demonic entities and humans with diabolical agendas hostile to the Kingdom of God.

If not for the *divine restraining orders* that will be issued from the Courts of Heaven, there are people who would be destroyed by the devil before they get their act together. Even in the natural world, a restraining or protective order is put in force to give the person in danger the time or space they need before they get a final ruling on the matter from the courts. However, a judge is the only person who can issue a restraining order. This is why the Lord wants you to accept the lifestyle of a judge in the Courts of Heaven so He can use you like Elijah to issue divine restraining orders on behalf of Heaven. *"And Elijah the Tishbite, of the inhabitants of Gilead, said to Ahab, 'As the Lord God of Israel lives, before whom I stand, there shall not be dew nor rain these years, except at my word'"* (1 Kings 17:1). I am still blown away by the fact that Joshua started out as a plaintiff but left as a judge with tremendous power in the Courts of Heaven. He was given a judicial seat among the "Cloud of Witnesses" and the 24 elders who are also judges in the Courts of Heaven.

Life Application
S E C T I O N

Memory Verse

Then he showed me Joshua the high priest standing before the Angel of the Lord, and Satan standing at his right hand to oppose him (Zechariah 3:1).

Reflections

1. Why is a godly lifestyle required for a believer to become an officer of the Courts of Heaven?

2. When you hear the word *iniquity*, what comes to your mind?

Chapter 6

The POWER *of*
a Spiritual Judge

*So Samuel grew, and the Lord was with him and let none
of his words fall to the ground.*

—1 Samuel 3:19

MAKING Joshua the high priest (see Zech. 3:7) into
one of the circuit judges in the Courts of Heaven carried serious implications. Joshua's judicial position in the
Courts of Heaven meant that if he passed judgment on anyone or
anything, God was for the most part obligated to honor his judgments
because he was an integral part of the heavenly circuit of judges. Concerning the prophet Samuel, I had always wondered why the Bible
says, *"The Lord was with him and let none of his words fall to the ground."*
Then a flash of revelation hit my spirit. The Lord showed me that
Samuel was more than a prophet; he had a heavenly judicial seat in
the Courts of Heaven. This means that his words carried the weight
of a prophet and judge. Wow! Check this out! *"And Samuel judged
Israel all the days of his life. He went from year to year on a circuit to*

Bethel, Gilgal, and Mizpah, and judged Israel in all those places" (1 Sam. 7:15-16). I believe that the Lord wants to raise many male and female "Samuels" in the Body of Christ using books like this one and Robert Henderson's *Operating in the Courts of Heaven.*

Do you know that one of the most difficult things that most courts of law don't enjoy doing is overturning the ruling of another judge? There is *judicial hesitancy* that is built into any judicial system when it comes to overruling the judgment of another judge.

Why? This is due to the fact that all governments want to protect the integrity of their judicial systems. However, there are instances when a judge botched a case so badly that if the higher or appeals court did not overturn the judge's ruling, the entire judicial system would be compromised. Can you imagine yourself coming into such a place of spiritual stature that even God Himself is reluctant to overturn what you decree? How powerful is that? This is what I believe happened when Elijah said, "for three years there will be no rain in Israel except at my word." The Scripture does not tell us that God told him to make this decree. Nevertheless, when he made this judicial decree, all of heaven went along with it! How many of us want to provide the Lord with the kind of lifestyle that would let Him allow us to do this?

Applying Divine Restraining Orders

I want to make a very important point here. We must not run around applying divine restraining orders over people and situations without giving God the lifestyle He requires for us to function in this type of judicial power in the Courts of Heaven. Only God knows your heart and lifestyle, so He is the only one who can give you a witness in your spirit whether you are still a plaintiff in the Courts of Heaven or a judge. *"The Spirit Himself bears witness with our spirit that we are children of God"* (Rom. 8:16). It would be quite presumptuous, even dangerous, to assume a judicial position in the Courts of Heaven without the direct witness of the Holy Spirit. Someone who has been qualified by God to function as a judge in the Courts of Heaven can apply divine restraining orders directly, without experiencing any demonic backlash whatsoever. The good news for the rest of us is simply this: *no matter the level of our spiritual maturity or lack thereof, if you are a blood-washed child of God, you can still come before the Righteous Judge and request that He apply a divine restraining order on your behalf or someone else's.*

In natural judicial systems, lawyers can go before a judge and request a restraining or protective order on behalf of their client. They can argue the merits of their case—why their client needs a restraining order from the court. However, no lawyer can unilaterally sign a restraining order on behalf of their clients because their status in the courtroom is not high enough to issue a restraining order. The restraining order must come directly from a judge. In a court-room, Judges are like kings. Kings carry or embody their "kingdom" wherever they go. In a similar fashion, judges carry or embody "the court" wherever they go. This is why a judge can turn a classroom into a courtroom by his or her presence. Whenever a judge walks into a room, he or she brings the court with them. When Apostle Robert Henderson was ministering at our church during a Courts of Heaven conference, I could literally sense the presence of the heavenly courtroom in our sanctuary. There have been many spiritual breakthroughs in our church since he led our people through the Courts of Heaven.

Jesus Functioning as Judge

Then the scribes and Pharisees brought to Him a woman caught in adultery. And when they had set her in the midst, they said to Him, "Teacher, this woman was caught in adultery, in the very act. Now Moses, in the law, commanded us that such should be stoned. But what do You say?" This they said, testing Him, that they might have something of which to accuse Him. But Jesus stooped down and wrote on the ground with His finger, as though He did not hear. So when they continued asking Him, He raised Himself up and said to them, "He who is without sin among you, let him throw a stone at her first." And again He stooped down and wrote on the ground. Then those who heard it, being convicted by their conscience went out one by one, beginning with the oldest even to the last. And Jesus was left alone, and the woman standing in the midst. When Jesus had raised Himself up and saw no one but the woman, He said to her, "Woman, where are those accusers of yours? Has no one condemned you?" She said, "No one, Lord." And Jesus said to her, "Neither do I condemn you; go and sin no more" (John 8:3-11).

In similar fashion, when God comes on the scene, He brings the heavenly courtroom with Him. God is the embodiment of the Courts of Heaven. This is why Jesus (God with us) could easily release the woman who was caught in adultery from being stoned to death. Even though He was on earth, He still retained His heavenly judicial seat as the Righteous Judge. Wherever He was, He brought the Courts of Heaven with Him. As soon as the Pharisees brought the woman who was caught in adultery to Him to pass judgment, the heavenly courtroom went into an emergency session. Even in natural judicial systems, the only time the courts go into an emergency session is when there is an urgent motion for a "stay of execution." In other words, the clock is ticking against somebody's life. This was the situation Jesus was placed in when the Pharisees cornered Him with this case. Thankfully for the woman caught in adultery, Jesus knew that He was both God and Judge.

The Pharisees pressed Him for an unrighteous verdict based upon a distorted understanding of the Law of Moses. Jesus simply looked down and wrote on the ground with His finger. I believe that the Lord Jesus was listening to His heavenly Father for a righteous verdict. When He finally passed judgment, something mind-boggling happened next. Without violating the Mosaic Law, Jesus demonstrated the true spirit of the law—*mercy triumphing over judgment*. He simply said, *"He who is without sin among you, let him throw a stone at her first."*

One by one the woman's accusers began to leave, from the oldest to youngest. The woman's eyes were probably closed, thinking the stone throwing would begin at any moment. She began to hear loud thuds as the stones began to hit the ground around her. The stones were falling, but none crashed down on her petrified body. When she finally gathered the courage to open her eyes, her accusers had disappeared. Relief flooded her soul, but she was not yet in the clear until the judge's final ruling. Herein lies the difference between divine restraining orders and the *final ruling* of a judge. Jesus imposed a *divine restraining order* on the *murderous spirit* of the woman's male accusers, but that was not enough to set her free. She needed the final ruling of the Righteous Judge (Jesus) in order to be truly free. Thankfully, He made His final ruling when He said:

> *"Woman, where are those accusers of yours? Has no one condemned you?" She said, "No one, Lord." And Jesus said to her, "Neither do I condemn you; go and sin no more."*

Life Application
S E C T I O N

Memory Verse

When Jesus had raised Himself up and saw no one but the woman, He said to her, "Woman, where are those accusers of yours? Has no one condemned you?" She said, "No one, Lord." And Jesus said to her, "Neither do I condemn you; go and sin no more" (John 8:10-11).

Reflections

1. Why are judges so important in a courtroom?

_____

_____

_____

_____

_____

2. How did Jesus deliver the woman who was caught in adultery?

_____

_____

_____

_____

_____

Chapter 7

Features of a DIVINE
Restraining Order

*And said, "O full of all deceit and all fraud, you son of
the devil, you enemy of all righteousness, will you not
cease perverting the straight ways of the Lord? And now,
indeed, the hand of the Lord is upon you, and you shall be
blind, not seeing the sun for a time." And immediately a
dark mist fell on him, and he went around seeking someone
to lead him by the hand. Then the proconsul believed,
when he saw what had been done, being astonished at the
teaching of the Lord.*

— Acts 13:10-12

W E will now begin to examine the *features* of *divine
restraining orders*. I want you to understand the features
of natural and spiritual restraining orders. I want to discuss the features of natural and spiritual restraining orders before I get
into biblical case studies for divine restraining orders. You will find
these biblical case studies very interesting indeed. Let us begin with a

statement from a legal dictionary about the general features of a natu-ral restraining or protective order. After we establish how restraining orders work in natural judicial systems, we'll move on to how divine restraining orders work within the Courts of Heaven.

> All restraining orders begin with an application to the court, which decides the merits of the request by using its traditional litmus test. Limited in their duration and effect, restraining orders are distinguished from the more lasting form of court intervention called an injunction. Generally, they are sought as a form of immediate relief while a plaintiff pursues a permanent injunction.

> A court submits a request for a restraining order to one of several tests. These tests vary slightly across different jurisdictions but generally they involve the analysis of four separate factors:
>
> 1. Whether the moving party will suffer irreparable injury if the relief is not granted;
>
> 2. Whether the moving party is likely to succeed on the merits of the case;
>
> 3. Whether the opposing party will be harmed more than the moving party is helped;
>
> 4. Whether granting the relief is in the public interest.

Usually, restraining orders are not permanent. They exist because of the need for immediate relief required by the plaintiff and the need for fast action from the court to prevent injury.[1]

Restraining orders are distinguished from the more lasting ruling of the courts called an injunction. As we have already stated, they are sought as a form of immediate relief while the plaintiff is in pursuit of a permanent solution.

It is important to take note that divine restraining orders, like their natural counterparts, are a temporal remedy to a spiritual problem that requires a permanent solution. Some Christians make the mistake of thinking *a divine restraining order equals complete deliverance.* They end up saying, "The Lord has delivered me," when in actuality all the Lord has done is impose a restraining order on the devil while His people get their act together. Some natural restraining orders last for only 90 days to a year. This is because the courts expect the plaintiff (you) to come before the court within the period of the restraining order to get a final injunction. For instance, the Lord gave the people of Israel time to get their act together while a divine restraining order was put in place against the Philistines during the days of Samuel (see 1 Sam. 7). Instead of getting their act together, the people of Israel were playing around until Samuel's death. Because the divine restraining order that kept the Philistines out of the land of Israel was connected to the life of Samuel, the Philistines attacked Israel immediately after the death of Samuel.

Legal Standing for
Restraining Orders

But they did not receive Him, because His face was set for the journey to Jerusalem. And when His disciples James and John saw this, they said, "Lord, do You want us to command fire to come down from heaven and consume them, just as Elijah did?" But He turned and rebuked them and said, "You do not know what manner of spirit you are of" (Luke 9:53-55).

I cannot overemphasize the fact that one of the most important issues that a court of law considers before taking on a case is the issue of *standing*. The issue of standing frees the court from being bogged down with frivolous lawsuits that have neither precedence nor merit. For instance, you cannot go down to the courthouse and ask the judge for a restraining order because your ex-husband is posting pictures of his new girlfriend on Facebook. The judge will run you out of his courtroom! Your ex-husband posting pictures of his new girlfriend on Facebook poses no physical danger to you or the public. These kinds of frivolous lawsuits lack both merit and imminent danger for the plaintiff. So, no self-respecting judge would ever issue a restraining order based upon such foolishness. The judge would remind you that his courtroom is not a reality show. So why would we expect God, the Righteous Judge, to issue divine restraining orders frivolously? There has to be real danger to your life, entity, or destiny before the Lord, the Righteous Judge, can sign off on issuing a divine restraining order on the behavior of your "ex." It cannot be issued on the basis that he is posting pictures of his new girlfriend on Facebook and it's making you really mad. That's not going to fly before a natural judge; why would it fly before the Judge of the whole earth?

As I have spent considerable time studying the subject of divine restraining orders, below are what I consider biblical reasons for requesting a divine restraining order from the Courts of Heaven.

> ## 1. Will the moving party (child of God) suffer irreparable damage or injury if the Courts of Heaven do not grant the divine restraining order?

Sometimes, God can see that you haven't got your act together. The Lord can see that the devil has legal standing against you. These are times when Satan has irrefutable evidence to destroy your destiny and even end your life. However your heavenly Father can see that you are at your wits' end spiritually, mentally, and emotionally, and if the merciful, Righteous Judge does not intervene with a divine restraining order to give you some immediate relief, Satan could score a permanent victory. So, the Holy Spirit will move on the heart of an officer of the Court in your proximity to get you a divine restraining order until you get your act together. This seems to have been what the Lord Jesus did for Peter. Satan came before the Courts of Heaven with irrefutable evidence that would have allowed him to sift or shake Peter up! However, our precious Lord became Peter's advocate before the Courts of Heaven and obtained a divine restraining order on Peter's behalf that limited the damage Satan could inflict upon Peter's person and destiny.

> *And the Lord said, "Simon, Simon! Indeed, Satan has asked for you, that he may sift you as wheat. But I have prayed for you, that your faith should not fail; and when you have returned to Me, strengthen your brethren"* (Luke 22:31-32).

2. Whether the moving party (child of God) is likely to succeed on the merits of the case.

Are you likely to succeed if you bring your request for a divine restraining order before the Courts of Heaven? In the example we used earlier, if you brought up the fact that your ex-husband was posting pictures of his new girlfriend on Facebook, would you prevail on that issue? You wouldn't succeed on that issue. It's too frivolous and self-serving, most especially when we come before our heavenly Righteous Judge who hates even garments spotted by the flesh. Consequently, when you are requesting a divine restraining order before the Courts of Heaven, it is important that the moving party (child of God) does so in accordance with the will of God and for God's own glory. *"Now this is the confidence that we have in Him, that if we ask anything according to His will, He hears us"* (1 John 5:14).

3. Whether the opposing party will be harmed if the moving party (child of God) is helped?

In other words, if the Courts of Heaven granted you a divine restraining order, would the other party (person or entity) be injured more than you are helped as a child of God? I love this litmus test because it ensures that the Courts do not grant restraining orders based upon personal vendettas, especially in cases where there is no imminent danger against the plaintiff posed by the other party.

> But they did not receive Him, because His face was set for
> the journey to Jerusalem. And when His disciples James and
> John saw this, they said, "Lord, do You want us command

down fire and consume them, just as Elijah did?" But He turned and rebuked them and said, "You do not know what manner of spirit you are of" (Luke 9:53-55).

I'm so glad that this passage is in the Bible. It demonstrates why the Courts of Heaven do not issue divine restraining orders frivolously. In the above passage, the people of Samaria had just rejected the Lord Jesus Christ. His disciples, James and John, saw this and got very upset. It would seem like they were embarrassed for the Lord, but in actuality it was their own religious pride that got tickled. In heartfelt rage, they asked Jesus for permission to *command down fire and consume the Samaritans!* They were actually calling for the genocide of an entire population over one error in judgment. Had the Courts of Heaven granted them the judgment they sought, thousands would've been destroyed without actually helping the disciples except for feeding their pride and ego. Jesus, as an officer of the Court of Heaven, rebuked them for plotting a miscarriage of justice.

4. Whether granting the divine restraining order is in the public interest.

God loves His people and the general public. The Bible declares, *"For God so loved the world that He gave His only begotten Son, that whoever believes in Him should not perish but have everlasting life"* (John 3:16). This verse implies that God would never issue a divine restraining order on behalf of any of His children that is not in the interest of the public good. This is also one of the reasons why the Lord has placed a pending divine restraining order on how much and how long the antichrist can persecute God's elect during the great tribulation.

And unless those days were shortened, no flesh would be saved; but for the elect's sake those days will be shortened (Matthew 24:22).

Jesus is telling us here that God has placed a divine restraining order on the number of days the antichrist can deceive and persecute God's children who will be alive during the great tribulation. Why? If those days were never shortened (limited), even God's elect would be lost.

5. Whether granting the divine restraining order preserves God's purpose and the integrity of His good name.

In my humble opinion, the easiest divine restraining orders to acquire before the Courts of Heaven are the ones that are designed to preserve God's eternal purpose and the integrity of His good name. The following scriptures speak to this important fact:

For My own sake, for My own sake, I will do it; for how should My name be profaned? And I will not give My glory to another (Isaiah 48:11).

For Zion's sake I will not hold My peace, and for Jerusalem's sake I will not rest, until her righteousness goes forth as brightness, and her salvation as a lamp that burns (Isaiah 62:1).

Now the Lord spoke to Paul in the night by a vision, "Do not be afraid, but speak, and do not keep silent; for I am with you, and no one will attack you to hurt you; for I have many people in this city" (Acts 18:9-10).

Features of Divine Restraining Orders

1. They are specific; they are never ambiguous.

2. They restrict a specific activity.

3. They are designed to restrict a person, business, nation, or a spiritual entity.

4. They are temporary judicial rulings of the Courts of Heaven on behalf of Kingdom citizens in dire need of emergency relief. We cannot and must not mistake a temporary ruling (restraining order) from the Courts of Heaven to mean that we have been fully delivered, unless the Holy Spirit gives us witness that the restraining order has morphed into a permanent injunction against the demonic powers on our behalf.

5. The judgment for violating divine restraining orders is always swiftly enforced in the form of emotional distress, financial loss, or tremendous personal suffering. In some instances, the penalty for violating a divine restraining order issued by the Courts of Heaven can even be physical death. I am going to give you biblical case studies where somebody in the Bible violated a divine restraining order and actually died because of it.

6. Divine restraining orders are only issued by the Courts

of Heaven by God, the Righteous Judge, the Lord Jesus Christ, or human judges of the Courts of Heaven (such as Samuel or Paul) who live in the favor of His presence because of their life of total obedience to God. The prophet Elijah quickly comes to mind: "God before whom I stand" is another way of Elijah saying, "I have a lifestyle and spiritual jurisdiction that allows me to stand before Him as a Judge" (see 1 Kings 17:1).

7. Divine restraining orders do not change the inherent nature of the person or demonic entity that is being restrained by the Courts of Heaven. For instance, the book of Revelation speaks of a pending divine restraining order that God will impose on Satan for 1,000 years. During this millennium dispensation, Satan will not be allowed to tempt anyone on earth. However, as soon as the divine restraining order expires, Satan will go right back to being the accuser of the brethren just as he was previously, proving my point that divine restraining orders are never designed to change the inherent nature of the opposing party.

> *Then I saw an angel coming down from heaven, having the key to the bottomless pit and a great chain in his hand. He laid hold of the dragon, that serpent of old, who is the Devil and Satan, and bound him for a thousand years; and he cast him into the bottomless pit, and shut him up, and set a seal on him, so that he should deceive the nations no more till the thousand years were finished. But after these things he must be released for a little while* (Revelation 20:1-3).

If your ex-husband is violent toward you, a divine restraining order will not change his violent nature. However, a divine restraining order will restrain his violent nature from manifesting in your presence. This is why you need to press into the Courts of Heaven until the Righteous Judge grants you a permanent injunction to protect you from your ex-husband's violent and abusive nature once the divine restraining order expires. However, while the divine restraining order is in effect, you can use this special time of relief to fast and pray for the Lord to grant you permanent deliverance.

8. In certain cases, divine restraining orders may apply to a specific territory or moment of time. This is why people experience spiritual breakthrough in certain "open heaven territories" that they cannot get anywhere else.

9. Divine restraining orders do not represent the anointing of the human person or angel applying them on behalf of the Courts of Heaven. Divine restraining orders represent the authority of the Courts of Heaven and the government that the Courts represent. This is why when you violate a restraining order in any country, you are challenging the authority of the court that issued it and the government it represents. This is why people seek them in the first place—because they know that restraining orders are fully enforceable.

10. The Holy Spirit is the most important officer of the Courts of Heaven in the matter of issuing divine restraining orders. In a few instances, the Holy Spirit imposed divine restraining orders on Paul's ministry excursions.

Now when they had gone through Phrygia and the region of Galatia, they were forbidden by the Holy Spirit to preach the word in Asia. After they had come to Mysia, they tried to go into Bithynia, but the Spirit did not permit them. So passing by Mysia, they came down to Troas (Acts 16:6-8).

Paul and Silas tried to preach in Asia and Bithynia; instead, the Holy Spirit imposed divine restraining orders on Paul's ministry to prevent him from going to these regions at that particular time. They could not go in and preach. It is not because the devil was stopping them but because there was a divine restraining order in place. Paul, being an obedient officer of the Courts of Heaven, did not dare to violate these divine restraining orders.

11. Violating a divine restraining order is equivalent to holding the Courts of Heaven in contempt. This is what is known as *contempt of court.* Every law-abiding nation carries stiff penalties for contempt of court violations. If a judge's restraining order is violated without penalty, the integrity of the entire judicial system is in danger of digressing into anarchy. The courts would lose stature before the general population. Think about this! If you can violate a restraining order and nothing happens to you, why can't the next guy do it, too? The entire judicial system of any country depends on the severity of the punishment for violating a judge's restraining order. So, why we would we expect the highest Court of appeal, the Courts of Heaven, to ignore violations of divine restraining orders issued from heavenly places?

Life Application
S E C T I O N

Memory Verse

"And now, indeed, the hand of the Lord is upon you, and you shall be blind, not seeing the sun for a time." And immediately a dark mist fell on him, and he went around seeking someone to lead him by the hand. Then the proconsul believed, when he saw what had been done, being astonished at the teaching of the Lord (Acts 13:11-12).

Reflections

1. Write down three features of a divine restraining order.

2. Why does a court of law demand you establish legal standing before a judge can issue you a restraining order?

Chapter 8

BIBLICAL *Case Studies*
of Divine Restraining Orders

> *Then she said to him, "How can you say, 'I love you,'*
> *when your heart is not with me? You have mocked me*
> *these three times, and have not told me where your great*
> *strength lies." And it came to pass, when she pestered*
> *him daily with her words and pressed him, so that his*
> *soul was vexed to death, that he told her all his heart, and*
> *said to her, "No razor has ever come upon my head, for I*
> *have been a Nazirite to God from my mother's womb. If*
> *I am shaven, then my strength will leave me, and I shall*
> *become weak, and be like any other man."*

—Judges 16:15-17

I N this chapter I will begin to give you some biblical case studies on the subject of divine restraining orders. These biblical case studies will help to establish the biblical framework for these divine restraining orders. They will also give you a clear picture of how divine restraining orders work in real time. These biblical case studies also create precedence for many of the "Prayers of Activation" in the last chapter of this book.

Case Study #1

Some divine restraining orders are designed to restrain demonic activity from crossing over into a geographical region for a short or extended period of time.

Let's now look at First Samuel 7:6-15 for our first biblical case study:

So they gathered together at Mizpah, drew water, and poured it out before the Lord. And they fasted that day, and said there, "We have sinned against the Lord." And Samuel judged the children of Israel at Mizpah. Now when the Philistines heard that the children of Israel had gathered together at Mizpah, the lords of the Philistines went up against Israel. And when the children of Israel heard of it, they were afraid of the Philistines. So the children of Israel said to Samuel, "Do not cease to cry out to the Lord our God for us, that He may save us from the hand of the Philistines."

And Samuel took a suckling lamb and offered it as a whole burnt offering to the Lord. Then Samuel cried out to the Lord for Israel, and the Lord answered him. Now as Samuel was offering up the burnt offering, the Philistines drew near to battle against Israel. But the Lord thundered with a loud thunder upon the Philistines that day, and so confused them that they were overcome before Israel. And the men of Israel went out of Mizpah and pursued the Philistines, and drove them back as far as below Beth Car. Then Samuel took a stone and set it up between Mizpah and Shen, and called its name Ebenezer, saying, "Thus far the Lord has helped us."

So the Philistines were subdued, and they did not come anymore into the territory of Israel. And the hand of the Lord was against the Philistines all the days of Samuel. Then the cities, which the Philistines had taken from Israel, were restored to Israel, from Ekron to Gath; and Israel recovered its territory from the hands of the Philistines. Also there was peace between Israel and the Amorites. And Samuel judged Israel all the days of his life (1 Samuel 7:6-15).

I have always been fascinated by the life of the prophet Samuel. Samuel functioned in three mantles as a *priest, prophet, and judge.* One thing I love about the Holy Spirit is that He uses the right terminology when he is trying to focus on a specific grace. Why would the Holy Spirit call Samuel a judge unless he was functioning as an officer of the Courts of Heaven within Israel's borders? The Bible declares, *"Samuel judged Israel all the days of his life. He went from year to year on a circuit to Bethel, Gilgal, and Mizpah, and judged Israel in all those places."* He judged Israel in these locations all the days of his life. Our current judicial systems also have "circuit judges" who function in similar fashion as Samuel; perhaps they borrowed this idea from the Bible.

The Bible tells us that there came a time when the Philistines chose to invade the nation of Israel. They were quite a formidable force, and the people of Israel were quite terrified of them. The Bible declares that the people of Israel cried to the Lord for deliverance and then went to see Samuel. Being a judge in the Courts of Heaven,

Samuel showed them the evidence that Satan had gathered against them in the Courts of Heaven that was giving him legal grounds to destroy the nation through the Philistines. When the people broke out into heartfelt repentance and destroyed idols of other gods, God gave them a favorable righteous verdict.

When the Philistines tried to attack Israel, the Lord thundered against them from the heavenly realms and began to fight on Israel's behalf. The battlefield configurations changed so rapidly, the Philistines were placed on the run. The children of Israel destroyed them while they were fleeing. Then something really powerful happened: *"So the Philistines were subdued, and they did not come anymore into the territory of Israel. And the hand of the Lord was against the Philistines all the days of Samuel."*

What just happened here? God imposed a divine restraining order on the Philistines all the days of Samuel—Samuel's life span was the time period allotted to this specific restraining order. The divine restraining order was such that the Philistines could never cross into Israel's territorial borders while Samuel was alive. The expression "all the days of Samuel" means that the divine restraining order was directly tied to Samuel's judicial seat in the Courts of Heaven while he was alive. The Lord showed me that He is raising Samuel-type apostolic and prophetic leaders who will be responsible for protecting entire regions from demonic invasion. We know that what kept the Philistines out of the borders of Israel was a *divine restraining order* because their inherent nature or hatred for Israel never changed, and yet they couldn't cross Israel's borders. Any attempt to cross the borders was met with immediate resistance from angels that were commissioned by God to enforce the divine restraining order that was connected to Samuel's judicial seat.

The Day of Samuel Type Leaders

So the Philistines were subdued, and they did not come any-
more into the territory of Israel. And the hand of the Lord
was against the Philistines all the days of Samuel (1 Samuel
7:13).

Check this out! The divine restraining order that was keeping the
Philistines out of Israel's territorial borders was connected to the life
of the judge—Samuel! This is why when Samuel-type leaders show
up in a region, certain demonic activities stop happening. The presence of these Samuel-type leaders acts as a temporary divine restraining order over the region. When Samuel died, the Philistines had the
right to return to Israel's borders because Samuel's death meant the
divine restraining order that kept them out of Israel's sovereign territory had expired. As soon as Samuel died, guess what happened? Israel
went to war with the Philistines several times until the Philistines
captured the Ark of God. What a travesty! Even though Samuel per-
sonally mentored King Saul, he never made a commitment to adopt
the same type of godly lifestyle that would have enabled the Lord to
give him Samuel's judicial seat in the Courts of Heaven after Samuel's
demise.

Consequently when Samuel died, his powerful judicial seat was
lost to Israel for a generation until King David's reign. David was
another spiritual son of Samuel; unlike King Saul, David had adopted
the same godly lifestyle and mantle as Samuel so he was able to legally
regain Samuel's judicial seat in the Courts of Heaven.

Now when the Philistines heard that they had anointed
David king over Israel, all the Philistines went up to search
for David. And David heard of it and went down to the

stronghold. The Philistines also went and deployed themselves in the Valley of Rephaim. So David inquired of the Lord, saying, "Shall I go up against the Philistines? Will You deliver them into my hand?" And the Lord said to David, "Go up, for I will doubtless deliver the Philistines into your hand." So David went to Baal Perazim, and David defeated them there; and he said, "The Lord has broken through my enemies before me, like a breakthrough of water." Therefore he called the name of that place Baal Perazim (2 Samuel 5:17-20).

The children of Israel never lost a battle to the Philistines all the days of King David.

From the Courtroom to the Battlefield

Another equally important facet of the story is that the children of Israel did not rush into a battlefield formation with the Philistines before they visited the heavenly Courtroom of Samuel's prophetic and judicial grace. This passage of Scripture proves Robert Henderson's thesis and teaching that "*if the body of Christ learns how to tackle much of our spiritual warfare in the heavenly courtroom, first and foremost, many of us may never need to go to the battlefield.*" On the other hand if you've been to the courtroom and presented your case before our heavenly Father, the Righteous Judge, you can go into your battlefield formation having already secured legal precedence for your time of warfare on the battlefield. The children of Israel went out of the courtroom when they pursued the Philistines. *Talk about a biblical pattern staring you right in the face!*

Samuel was very disappointed when God rejected Saul because Samuel had hoped Saul would inherit his judicial seat in the Courts of Heaven. When Samuel realized his judicial seat would not be transferred to Saul, he knew intuitively what was going to happen to the nation after his death. The Philistines would return with a vengeance. Saul and the people of Israel would go back to the battlefield to face the Philistines because the divine restraining order would be rescinded. This is why the Lord sent David to live with Samuel at Ramah so he could train him on how to function as a priest, prophet, and judge. This is why David was able to function in all the "anointings" of Samuel.

Case Study #2

Some divine restraining orders are designed to restrain people's behavior within a specific distance.

So David fled and escaped, and went to Samuel at Ramah, and told him all that Saul had done to him. And he and Samuel went and stayed in Naioth. Now it was told Saul, saying, "Take note, David is at Naioth in Ramah!" Then Saul sent messengers to take David. And when they saw the group of prophets prophesying, and Samuel standing as leader over them, the Spirit of God came upon the messengers of Saul, and they also prophesied. And when Saul was told, he sent other messengers, and they prophesied likewise. Then Saul sent messengers again the third time, and they prophesied also. Then he also went to Ramah, and came to the great well that is at Sechu. So he asked, and said, "Where are Samuel and David?" And someone said,

"Indeed they are at Naioth in Ramah." So he went there to Naioth in Ramah. Then the Spirit of God was upon him also, and he went on and prophesied until he came to Naioth in Ramah. And he also stripped off his clothes and prophesied before Samuel in like manner, and lay down naked all that day and all that night. Therefore they say, "Is Saul also among the prophets?" (1 Samuel 19:18-24)

There was another life-changing divine restraining order that was connected to the life of Samuel. This divine restraining order worked in such a way that when a person with a demonic agenda got anywhere near Samuel, the demonic nature inside of them would be completely restrained and replaced with a God-glorifying prophetic spirit. Wow! We definitely need this type of divine restraining order to begin to function within the Body of Christ. Why? We are living in dangerous times as the end of this present age of sin rapidly approaches. The devil is pulling out all the stops because he knows that his time is short! Plus, you never know who enters your sanctuary or home.

In Charleston, South Carolina, a white racist by the name of Dylann Roof entered the sanctuary of an AME Zion Church during their Wednesday night Bible study with the intent to kill. It is a shame when someone can walk into a church and shoot down the pastor. When everything was said and done, Dylann Roof had killed nine innocent people, including the church's senior pastor. There is something seriously wrong in the spiritual climate of any church when a demoniac can enter and do the devil's bidding without prophetic intercessors picking up on it! What if the spiritual climate of the church in Charleston was armed with the same kind of divine restraining order that was upon the life of Samuel?

The divine restraining order that was upon Samuel's life could change and restrain human behavior in a moment's notice. Samuel functioned in this kind of spiritual dimension. Not only did his judicial seat in the Courts of Heaven restrain territorial demons from violating Israel's sovereign borders, he had another kind of divine restraining order that could "restrain" human and demonic behavior when anybody came *within striking distance*. I have included a prayer of activation in the last chapter of this book to help you apply for this kind of divine restraining order in the Courts of Heaven so the Lord can release this type of grace over your church, place of business, or home.

Destiny Shelters!

It goes without saying that a demon of murder had possessed the soul of King Saul. Saul had become a demoniac. He was consumed with jealousy and hatred. On three separate occasions he tried to kill David with a javelin. David knew if he did not run away, death would soon become his portion. David knew, "My time in the king's palace is over! If I want to stay alive, I need to run." So what did David do? The Holy Spirit told David to find shelter under Samuel's priestly, prophetic, and judicial mantle.

I am convinced that God is raising Samuel-type apostolic and prophetic leaders who will function as *destiny shelters* for Davids in the Body of Christ who are running from demonic technologies and agendas that are hell-bent on destroying them before their God-given destinies can come forth. There are Davids in the global Body of Christ who desperately need the spiritual covering of these Samuel-type leaders before they come into their God-given destiny. The divine restraining order around these Samuel-type leaders will help keep this "David Company" alive to benefit the next generation. There are many Davids in our churches who are dying prematurely or losing their grip on destiny before their appointed time. Where are the Samuels who can protect these future leaders from being destroyed by the *Saul-spirit*? These demonic entities want to kill them before they come into their kingship.

Check this out! King Saul sent professional assassins to neutralize David. They all left with the intent to kill David. They left with premeditated murder on their minds. But when they came around Samuel and his group of prophets, the Spirit of God came upon the assassins. They all began to prophesy. The *divine restraining order* on Samuel's life as a judge was so strong it transformed hardcore killers into prophets. When Saul was told about what transpired, he became very angry. He sent more assassins and the same thing happened to them, too!

Resisting Arrest!

Finally King Saul said, "I am not going to trust anybody! I am going to kill him myself!" King Saul also went to Ramah where Samuel lived. As soon as he got within striking distance, *the divine restraining order was activated* and the Spirit of God came upon him also. Can you imagine King Saul trying to resist his heart turning soft toward David? He was probably saying to himself, "No! No! I'm not going to prophesy! I came here to kill David!" Unfortunately for him, the divine restraining order was so strong the demonic agenda in his heart was completely restrained. Knowing that the Lord has such a sense of humor, King Saul's prophetic utterance probably sounded like this: "The Lord says to you, David: you are a man after the heart of God and the Lord will establish your throne over Israel forever." If I were David, I would probably say something like this: "Amen brother!"

King Saul was trying to resist the divine restraining order so much so that God *stripped him naked just to humble him*. You see, the stronger you resist a divine restraining order, the more you incite the Courts of Heaven to prove to you the power of the heavenly Courtroom. All of Saul's assassins were subdued with prophecy, but Saul was subdued by public embarrassment. *He went down naked and prophesied all day and night.* Can you imagine the sight of a butt-naked king prophesying in the streets while all the children and his loyal citizens watched the grand spectacle play out? I don't know about you but the sight of a naked man prophesying in the streets for hours would send me into professional therapy. I'm sure there were little children who were traumatized by what they saw!

Case Study #3

Some divine restraining orders are designed to restrain the satanic activities of a person who stands in the way of the gospel of the Lord Jesus Christ.

Now when they had gone through the island to Paphos, they found a certain sorcerer, a false prophet, a Jew whose name was Bar-Jesus, who was with the proconsul, Sergius Paulus, an intelligent man. This man called for Barnabas and Saul and sought to hear the word of God. But Elymas the sorcerer (for so his name is translated) withstood them, seeking to turn the proconsul away from the faith. Then Saul, who also is called Paul, filled with the Holy Spirit, looked intently at him and said, "O full of all deceit and all fraud, you son of the devil, you enemy of all righteousness, will you not cease perverting the straight ways of the Lord? And now, indeed, the hand of the Lord is upon you, and you shall be blind, not seeing the sun for a time." And

> *immediately a dark mist fell on him, and he went around seeking someone to lead him by the hand. Then the proconsul believed, when he saw what had been done, being astonished at the teaching of the Lord* (Acts 13:6-12).

In the thirteenth chapter of Acts, the Lord introduces us to another kind of divine restraining order that really excites me. Paul and Barnabas were sent on an apostolic assignment to an island called Paphos. The governor or proconsul of this little island was a man by the name of *Sergius Paulus*. Apparently, this man was very open to the gospel of the Kingdom that Paul and Barnabas preached. However, a sorcerer and false prophet by the name of *Bar-Jesus*, who served as a spiritual advisor to the proconsul, was actively engaged in resisting the preaching of the gospel. Paul, being an officer of the Courts of Heaven and apostle, was ticked off by this man's behavior.

Stepping into his judicial seat, Paul imposed a divine restraining order against this messenger of Satan who was standing in the way of the gospel. Why would Paul, the apostle, impose a divine restraining order on this man if he did not occupy a judicial seat in the Courts of Heaven? We have already established the fact that in any judicial system, restraining orders can only be applied by a judge's order.

What is also interesting about this particular divine restraining order is that Paul took the time to establish legal standing before the Courts of Heaven before he imposed this special divine restraining order on Bar-Jesus. Paul proved that:

1. Bar-Jesus was full of all deceit;

2. Bar-Jesus was full of all fraud;

3. Bar-Jesus was the son of the devil;

4. Bar-Jesus was an enemy of all righteousness;

5. Bar-Jesus was not going to cease perverting the straight ways of the Lord.

After proving that he had legal standing before the Courts of Heaven to impose a divine restraining order on Bar-Jesus, he went ahead and issued it! Here comes the *divine restraining order*:

> *And now, indeed, the hand of the Lord is upon you, and you shall be blind, not seeing the sun for a time* (Acts 13:11).

Please take note that as with all divine restraining orders, their purpose is never to change the inherent nature of the opposing party but rather to restrain the opposing party from causing any further damage. When Paul imposed this divine restraining order, his decree made it very clear that it was only "for a time." Paul's divine restraining order superimposed a spirit of blindness on Bar-Jesus. The Bible says immediately a dark mist fell on Bar-Jesus and he went around seeking someone to lead him by the hand. And when the proconsul saw this he was astonished! He quickly gave his life to the Lord. I believe that there will be evangelists and missionaries who are going to operate mightily in this type of divine restraining order for the furtherance of the gospel. God is going to use them to open up entire regions to the gospel of Jesus Christ. I believe that this type of divine restraining order will come in handy as God opens doors for mass evangelistic crusades in predominantly Muslim nations and regions held captive by the spirit of religion and witchcraft.

Case Study #4

The highest divine restraining order in the Courts of Heaven is the one that restrains Lucifer himself.

Then the Lord said to Satan, "Have you considered My servant Job, that there is none like him on the earth, a blameless and upright man, one who fears God and shuns evil?" So Satan answered the Lord and said, "Does Job fear God for nothing? Have You not made a hedge around him, around his household, and around all that he has on every side? You have blessed the work of his hands, and his possessions have increased in the land. But now, stretch out Your hand and touch all that he has, and he will surely curse You to Your face!" And the Lord said to Satan, "Behold, all that he has is in your power; only do not lay a hand on his person." So Satan went out from the presence of the Lord (Job 1:8-12).

Our final biblical case study of divine restraining orders brings us to the highest divine restraining order that can ever be issued from the Courts of Heaven. *The Lord Himself, our Righteous Judge, is the only one who can apply this type of divine restraining order.* I have heard overzealous intercessors say "we bind the devil, we send him right now to the bottomless pit." Fact check: There is no human being this side of heaven who can send Lucifer (Satan) into the bottomless pit. Why? Satan still has work to do that is directly connected to God's manifold wisdom to conclude and consummate this present age of sin in Christ Jesus. Even a high-ranking archangel like Michael had to make an appeal to the Righteous Judge (the Lord) in order to arm wrestle the body of Moses from Satan's legal claim.

> *Yet Michael the archangel, in contending with the devil, when he disputed about the body of Moses, dared not bring against him a reviling accusation, but said, "The Lord rebuke you!"* (Jude 1:9)

It is important for us to know this! When dealing with Lucifer (Satan), we have authority over the devil through Christ our Lord. However, the best way to contend with Satan is to bind him in the Courts of Heaven. In legal terminology, *binding* means *to restrict or restrain.* This is what the Lord Jesus had in mind when He said, *"Assuredly, I say to you, whatever you bind on earth will be bound in heaven, and whatever you loose on earth will be loosed in heaven"* (Matt. 18:18). Jesus was not thinking of battleground warfare when He told us to bind and loose. *He was referencing and envisioning a courtroom drama.* The terms He uses here are all legal terms courts all over the world use in the practice of law.

In the first chapter of Job, verses 6 to 12, Satan appears before the Courts of Heaven to present caseloads of evidence against the inhabitants of the earth that he had collected by walking "to and fro" across multiple generational lines. Satan appears before the Court in his traditional role as "accuser." The Lord says to him, "Have you considered my servant Job?" The expression "considered" used in the text means "to investigate." Satan quickly responds and tells the Lord, "Job only serves You because of the things You have given him. You let me touch him and You will see that he is not really into You." In response to Satan's accusation, the Lord does something very interesting. He grants the devil permission to touch Job's property and family but the Lord imposes a divine restraining order on Satan.

God says, in actuality, "Satan, you can touch everything he has except take his life." This means that no matter what the devil did to Job, he couldn't kill Job without violating the divine restraining order imposed on him by the Court of Heaven. *The divine restraining order God placed on Satan to protect Job was so powerful, you could shoot Job in the head and he wouldn't die.* In the final chapter of this book under "Prayers of Activation," I will show you how to apply for a divine restraining order against premature death. *I am coming into a covenantal agreement with you that you will not die before your appointed time!* Can you imagine living with a divine restraining order that protects you from every manner of premature death? Like Bishop Tudor Bismarck would say, "The devil and his mother-in-law can never take your life if he tried." That's simply amazing!

Life Application
S E C T I O N

Memory Verse

And it came to pass, when she pestered him daily with her words and pressed him, so that his soul was vexed to death, that he told her all his heart, and said to her, "No razor has ever come upon my head, for I have been a Nazirite to God from my mother's womb. If I am shaven, then my strength will leave me, and I shall become weak, and be like any other man" (Judges 16:16-17).

Reflections

1. Write down two biblical case studies where a divine restraining order was imposed.

2. What kind of divine restraining order did the Lord impose on Satan as it relates to Job?

Chapter 9

The Purpose of DIVINE Restraining Orders

Many plans are in a man's mind, but it is the Lord's purpose for him that will stand (be carried out).

—Proverbs 19:21 AMP

TWO of my favorite Bible teachers since I came to Christ are the late Dr. Myles Munroe and Ravi Zacharias. In Christendom, Dr. Myles Munroe was one of the most prolific Bible teachers on the subject of purpose. Every time I pick up Dr. Myles Munroe's book *In Pursuit of Purpose,* I am awestruck by the sense of divine destiny that consumes me. Dr. Myles Munroe defined "purpose" as *the primary motivation or original intent in the mind of the manufacturer for the creation of a product.* One thing that is abundantly clear is that God is a God of purpose! Everything God does has a purpose and is driven by the desire to achieve that purpose.

In this chapter, we will zero in on God's purpose for issuing divine restraining orders, which ones to apply, where, and when. This chapter will give us a broader spectrum on the whole subject of *issuing divine restraining orders from the Courts of Heaven!*

1. Protecting Territory

Some divine restraining orders are designed to restrain demonic "activity" from crossing over into a specific and divinely protected geographical territory. For instance, in First Samuel 7, the Philistines couldn't cross any of Israel's borders all the days of the prophet Samuel's life. The strength of Samuel's mantle as priest, prophet, and judge (officer of the Courts of Heaven) combined with his ability to cooperate with the Holy Spirit made it impossible for the enemies of Israel to violate its sovereign borders.

> *So the Philistines were subdued, and they did not come anymore into the territory of Israel. And the hand of the Lord was against the Philistines all the days of Samuel. Then the cities which the Philistines had taken from Israel were restored to Israel, from Ekron to Gath; and Israel recovered its territory from the hands of the Philistines. Also there was peace between Israel and the Amorites. And Samuel judged Israel all the days of his life* (1 Samuel 7:13-15).

2. Restraining Ungodly Behavior

Some divine restraining orders are designed to restrain demonically engineered behavior in people who are within a specified distance from a sanctified human officer of the Courts of Heaven. In First Samuel 19, when King Saul sent professional assassins to kill David when he was taking shelter in Samuel's house in Ramah, these hardcore killers ended up prophesying and joining David instead of carrying out the king's command to spill David's blood. King Saul himself ended up being stripped naked in public when he tried to violate this divine restraining order that was upon Samuel's life.

Then he also went to Ramah, and came to the great well that is at Sechu. So he asked, and said, "Where are Samuel and David?" And someone said, "Indeed they are at Naioth in Ramah." So he went there to Naioth in Ramah. Then the Spirit of God was upon him also, and he went on and prophesied until he came to Naioth in Ramah. And he also stripped off his clothes and prophesied before Samuel in like manner, and lay down naked all that day and all that night. Therefore they say, "Is Saul also among the prophets?" (1 Samuel 19:22-24)

3. Restraining Enemies of the Gospel

Some divine restraining orders are designed to restrain the satanic activities of a person who stands in the way of the propagation of the gospel of the Lord Jesus Christ. In the Great Commission, Jesus made it clear that teaching this gospel of the Kingdom and discipling nations is the primary mandate of the New Testament church. Anything that stands in the way of this assignment is the spirit of the antichrist. In the book of Acts, Paul the apostle imposed a very severe *divine restraining order* on a sorcerer by the name of Bar-Jesus or Elymas by translation. A spirit of blindness came upon him and he started groping in the dark immediately, looking for someone to guide him along. The proconsul saw this and gladly gave his life to the Lord.

> *Now when they had gone through the island to Paphos, they found a certain sorcerer, a false prophet, a Jew whose name was Bar-Jesus, who was with the proconsul, Sergius Paulus, an intelligent man. This man called for Barnabas and Saul and sought to hear the word of God. But Elymas the sorcerer (for so his name is translated) withstood them, seeking to turn the proconsul away from the faith. Then Saul, who also is called Paul, filled with the Holy Spirit, looked intently at him and said, "O full of all deceit and all fraud, you son of the devil, you enemy of all righteousness, will you not cease perverting the straight ways of the Lord? And now, indeed, the hand of the Lord is upon you, and you shall be blind, not seeing the sun for a time." And immediately a dark mist fell on him, and he went around seeking someone to lead him by the hand. Then the proconsul believed, when he saw what had been done, being astonished at the teaching of the Lord* (Acts 13:6-12).

4. Restraining Satan

We have already determined that the highest divine restraining order is the one that in actuality restrains Lucifer/the devil himself. The Lord, as our Righteous Judge, is the only one who can apply this kind of divine restraining order. The book of Revelation tells us about a time that is rapidly approaching when Satan is going to be restrained or bound with a chain inside the bottomless pit for 1,000 years. During this millennial reign of Christ, nations will flourish spiritually and economically under the righteous reign of the Son of God. According to Bible prophecy, the Lord Jesus will sit and rule on the throne of David in Jerusalem for 1,000 years. Nations will come and pay homage to Him during the Feast of Tabernacles. But the Bible declares that after 1,000 years, the divine restraining order on Satan will be rescinded. Immediately after Satan's release from the awesome power of this divine restraining order, he will begin to tempt the inhabitants of the earth just like he used to before.

> *Then I saw an angel coming down from heaven, having the key to the bottomless pit and a great chain in his hand. He laid hold of the dragon, that serpent of old, who is the Devil and Satan, and bound him for a thousand years; and he cast him into the bottomless pit, and shut him up, and set a seal on him, so that he should deceive the nations no more till the thousand years were finished. But after these things he must be released for a little while* (Revelation 20:1-3).

5. Restraining Orders on God's Servants

Some divine restraining orders are designed to restrain the behavior of special servants of God who carry very strategic and critical Kingdom assignments. *These kinds of divine restraining orders are designed and imposed by God Himself.* In most cases, these divine restraining orders are God's *predetermined price* for carrying a special anointing, calling, or Kingdom mandate. In cases such as these, the violation of these *special divine restraining orders* can cost a man or woman of God with the special anointing, calling, status, or Kingdom assignment in which the Lord had predetermined for them to walk in. In most cases, when a high-profile man or woman of God whom the Lord was using mightily in the Body of Christ falls from grace, it is usually because they became undisciplined in maintaining the divine restraining order that God imposed upon their life in order for them to maintain their special anointing, status, calling, or Kingdom assignment.

In First Kings 13 there is an interesting story about a man of God who was sent by the Lord with an urgent message for the altar in Bethel and King Jeroboam. This man of God was sent by God to prophesy against the altar of Baal. He also prophesied about the supernatural birth of King Josiah 100 years before the child was actually born. When the man of God turned around to leave, King Jeroboam tried to attack him. Instead, the king's hand froze in midair. The king begged the man of God to pray to the Lord for his deliverance. The nameless man of God prayed and God healed the king's hand instantly. When the man of God turned to leave a second time, the king begged him to come to the palace and eat some food. The king's request triggered an amazing response. The man of God told the king about the *divine restraining order* that God had placed over his life and ministry. The man of God clearly defined what the *divine restraining order over his life was all about.* This is what happened:

> Then the king said to the man of God, "Come home with me and refresh yourself, and I will give you a reward." But the man of God said to the king, "If you were to give me half your house, I would not go in with you; nor would I eat bread nor drink water in this place. For so it was commanded me by the word of the Lord, saying, 'You shall not eat bread, nor drink water, nor return by the same way you came.'" So he went another way and did not return by the way he came to Bethel (1 Kings 13:7-10).

The Conditions of the Divine Restraining Order

1. He was not to eat bread in the city where he prophesied;

2. He was not to drink water in the city where he prophesied;

3. He was not allowed to use the same road he used coming into the city on his departure.

The conditions of this man's divine restraining order seemed simple enough. The conditions were clearly laid out. He knew them and also knew that maintaining the divine restraining order that God had placed over his life and ministry was the only way to maintain the special anointing, calling, status, or Kingdom assignment the Lord had placed upon his life. However, things are never that simple when the devil knows that there is a divine restraining order that maintains your special calling in the Kingdom of God. The devil will do everything in his power to tempt you to violate the divine restraining order that sustains and holds together your strategic calling in the Kingdom of God.

Before the nameless man of God left the city, an old prophet heard about the man of God's special visit and prophecy against the altar. The old prophet saddled his donkey and went after him. When the old prophet found the young prophet he told him a lie. He said to him:

> *Then he said to him, "Come home with me and eat bread."
> And he said, "I cannot return with you nor go in with you;
> neither can I eat bread nor drink water with you in this
> place. For I have been told by the word of the Lord, 'You
> shall not eat bread nor drink water there, nor return by
> going the way you came.'" He said to him, "I too am a
> prophet as you are, and an angel spoke to me by the word of
> the Lord, saying, 'Bring him back with you to your house,*

that he may eat bread and drink water.'" (He was lying to
him.) So he went back with him, and ate bread in his house,
and drank water (1 Kings 13:15-19).

This is a really sad story but this story is also a warning for servants of God who carry special assignments in the Kingdom. *Just because other people (Christians) can act a certain way does not mean that you can act the same way.* Your special calling from God may require a different type of divine restraint and lifestyle. As soon as the nameless man of God ate bread and drank the water in the house of the old lying prophet, his very promising ministry and life were suddenly cut short. *How ironic that the Lord used the same lying prophet who deceived him to pronounce his sentence.* When the young prophet left the old prophet's house, a lion killed him on his way home. Wow! Has the Lord made you aware of any divine restraining order that governs the special calling He has placed upon your life?

6. Restraining the Spirit of Premature Death

Some divine restraining orders are designed to restrain the spirit of death from taking people of destiny before their appointed time. Dr. Myles Munroe was famous for saying. "Death before the completion of your purpose is murder." I completely agree. God gave us the gift of physical life so that we can spend it on manifesting the God-given destiny He placed in our spirit before we were placed inside our mother's womb. Our physical life is the currency of spiritual destiny. If a person dies, their spirit leaves the body and this earth. We already know that spirits without physical bodies of dirt are illegal here on earth. *The Lord placed a divine restraining order on Satan to stop him from taking Job's physical life.* The Lord was not interested in having Job die before his appointed time (see Job 1:12).

The devil tried to shorten Paul's life by viciously attacking the cargo ship that was transporting him to Rome. However, he had a divine appointment with Caesar. The Lord had already told Paul the apostle that he wanted him to stand before Caesar so he could testify about the gospel of the Lord Jesus Christ. But the devil had enough of Paul. He was tired of seeing men like Paul turn the whole world upside down. So when the cargo ship was caught in a bad storm, the devil began to look for an opportunity to kill Paul prematurely. Unfortunately for the devil, an angel of the Lord appeared to Paul on the cargo ship to let him know that the Lord had just imposed a divine restraining order over his life against any form of premature death. The divine restraining order against premature death that the Lord placed on Paul the apostle also affected everybody who was on the cargo ship with him. Isn't the Lord so wonderful? The divine restraining order did not cover the loss of the ship's cargo.

> *And now I urge you to take heart, for there will be no loss of life among you, but only of the ship. For there stood by me this night an angel of the God to whom I belong and whom I serve, saying, "Do not be afraid, Paul; you must be brought before Caesar; and indeed God has granted you all those who sail with you." Therefore take heart, men, for I believe God that it will be just as it was told me* (Acts 27:22-25).

7. To Restrain Mother Nature

Some divine restraining orders are designed to restrain Mother Nature or the elements in our galaxy from interfering with the purposes of God or destroying people, food, and property. When God created man in the Garden of Eden, He gave them a powerful dominion mandate. Man's dominion mandate is quite large in scope. What is not in doubt is that God gave man dominion over this planet as well as the solar system. They say the proof is in the pudding—both Jesus and Elijah were able to restrain Mother Nature during their earthly ministry. Jesus spoke to a storm that was threatening to capsize His boat. On the other hand, Elijah imposed a divine restraining order against Mother Nature decreeing that it would not rain for three years until he said so (see 1 Kings 17). Joshua imposed one of the most powerful divine restraining orders against Mother Nature.

When Joshua was taking territory in the Promised Land, he realized that he needed more daytime to finish his assignment. Unfortunately, the sun was disappearing quickly, threatening to blanket them in the darkness of the night. Joshua would have none of it. So he spoke to both the sun and the moon and placed a divine restraining order on both of their movements for a short period of time. This resulted in Joshua ending up with a longer day than usual. As a result, Joshua was able to completely defeat his enemies. I believe that the Lord is about to raise Joshua-type leaders in the last days who will have supernatural faith to impose divine restraining orders on Mother Nature, especially when she's threatening to compromise or delay the purposes of God. These Joshua-type leaders will save governments from spending billions of dollars on disaster relief by stopping storms and hurricanes before they make landfall.

Then Joshua spoke to the Lord in the day when the Lord
delivered up the Amorites before the children of Israel, and
he said in the sight of Israel: "Sun, stand still over Gibeon;
and Moon, in the Valley of Aijalon." So the sun stood still,
and the moon stopped, till the people had revenge upon their
enemies. Is this not written in the Book of Jasher? So the sun
stood still in the midst of heaven, and did not hasten to go
down for about a whole day (Joshua 10:12-13).

8. Restrain the Righteous from Sinning

Some divine restraining orders are designed to protect the righteous from sinning against God. This divine restraining order is one of my favorites. The following story illustrates why this kind of divine restraining order is very important to preserve innocent people who are placed in compromising situations without their knowledge.

But God came to Abimelech in a dream by night, and said
to him, "Indeed you are a dead man because of the woman
whom you have taken, for she is a man's wife." But Abi-
melech had not come near her; and he said, "Lord, will You
slay a righteous nation also? Did he not say to me, 'She is my
sister'? And she, even she herself said, 'He is my brother.'
In the integrity of my heart and innocence of my hands I
have done this." And God said to him in a dream, "Yes, I
know that you did this in the integrity of your heart. For I
also **withheld you** [restrained you] *from sinning against*
Me; therefore I did not let you touch her. Now therefore,
restore the man's wife; for he is a prophet, and he will pray

for you and you shall live. But if you do not restore her, know that you shall surely die, you and all who are yours" (Genesis 20:3-7).

In the above passage, Abraham places a righteous king by the name of Abimelech in a very compromising situation. Out of his own sense of panic, Abraham was less than truthful when he introduced his wife Sarah to Abimelech. He told him that she was his natural sister. Because Abimelech was very attracted to her physically, he took her to his palace so he could marry her. There was only one problem! She was already married. Instantly, *the Lord imposed a divine restraining order on Abimelech's sexual desire for Sarah.* Instead of taking her directly to bed, Abimelech never touched her physically.

When he went to bed that night, the Lord appeared to him in a dream and exposed Abraham's deception. The Lord told Abimelech that if he did not restore Sarah to Abraham, God would kill him. Check out this conversation between God and Abimelech:

> *"Did he not say to me, 'She is my sister'? And she, even she herself said, 'He is my brother.' In the integrity of my heart and innocence of my hands I have done this." And God said to him in a dream, "Yes, I know that you did this in the integrity of your heart. **For I also withheld [restrained] you from sinning against Me; therefore I did not let you touch her.**"*

Can you imagine this? God told a righteous Gentile king that He had placed a divine restraining order on him in order to deliver him from sinning against God. How many of you would like the Lord to place this kind of divine restraining order on your life? This is why I love this kind of divine restraining order. In the last chapter under

"Prayers of Activation," I will show you how to apply for this kind of divine restraining order over your life.

9. To Preserve Destiny or God's Purpose

Some divine restraining orders are applied by angels or human officers of the Courts of Heaven in order to preserve the destiny or purposes of God. We see this type of divine restraining order when the angel Gabriel appeared to Zacharias. The angel Gabriel came to announce the miraculous birth of John the Baptist through his previously barren wife, Elizabeth. The angel Gabriel told Zacharias the good news, but there was only one problem—Zacharias had a difficult time believing it. When he opened his mouth, his doubts and unbelief spewed out of his mouth. Realizing that his mouth would endanger the fulfillment of God's purpose, the angel Gabriel imposed a divine restraining order over his mouth until the birth of the miracle baby.

> *And Zacharias said to the angel, "How shall I know this? For I am an old man, and my wife is well advanced in years." And the angel answered and said to him, "I am Gabriel, who stands in the presence of God, and was sent to speak to you and bring you these glad tidings. But behold, you will be mute and not able to speak until the day these things take place, because you did not believe my words which will be fulfilled in their own time"* (Luke 1:18-20).

Zacharias did not speak for nine months until the baby was born. When the baby was born, there was a family dispute over the name of the baby. Elizabeth named him John like the angel Gabriel had instructed them. But some family remembers were protesting the name. They finally looked to Zacharias to cast the final vote. They gave him a writing pad. As soon as he wrote down the name "John," the divine restraining order against his mouth was rescinded. Immediately, he began to prophesy. He was no longer spewing unbelief. He was in complete agreement with the purposes of God.

> So they made signs to his father—what he would have him called. And he asked for a writing tablet, and wrote, saying, "His name is John." So they all marveled. Immediately his mouth was opened and his tongue loosed, and he spoke, praising God (Luke 1:62-64).

10. Restraining Sexual Predators

> But the Lord plagued Pharaoh and his house with great plagues because of Sarai, Abram's wife. And Pharaoh called Abram and said, "What is this you have done to me? Why did you not tell me that she was your wife? Why did you say, 'She is my sister'? I might have taken her as my wife. Now therefore, here is your wife; take her and go your way" (Genesis 12:17-19).

Some divine restraining orders are designed to protect God's children from sexual predators in sexually promiscuous environments. This is an interesting divine restraining order. I believe it will be much needed in the last days as sexual promiscuity becomes rampant in our culture, in the corridors of government, the marketplace, and even in the church. (The recent nationwide sexual scandal involving iconic movie director Harvey Weinstein and many of the women he raped violently has shocked America and shaken the entire Hollywood entertainment industry.) The Lord used this kind of divine restraining order to protect Sarah from a lustful Egyptian king who wanted to violate her sexually. This divine restraining order against Pharaoh manifested itself in the form of plagues in his palace. So much so that he couldn't wait to get her out of his palace and restore her to Abraham.

> *Now before they lay down, the men of the city, the men of Sodom, both old and young, all the people from every quarter, surrounded the house. And they called to Lot and said to him, "Where are the men who came to you tonight? Bring them out to us that we may know them carnally." So Lot went out to them through the doorway, shut the door behind him, and said, "Please, my brethren, do not do so wickedly! See now, I have two daughters who have not known a man; please, let me bring them out to you, and you may do to them as you wish; only do nothing to these men, since this is the reason they have come under the shadow of my roof." And they said, "Stand back!" Then they said, "This one came in to stay here, and he keeps acting as a judge; now we will deal worse with you than with them." So they pressed hard against the man Lot, and came near to break down the door. But the men reached out their hands and pulled Lot into the house with them, and shut the door. And they struck the men who were at the doorway of the house with blindness, both small and great, so that they became weary trying to find the door* (Genesis 19:4-11).

The Lord also used this same kind of divine restraining order to protect Lot's virgin daughters from being raped by a mob of lustful men in Sodom who wanted to have sexual relations with the (male) angels who had entered into Lot's house. Lot was about to throw his daughters to this mob of sexual predators. Thankfully, the angels intervened. They opened the door and imposed the same divine restraining order on the men of Sodom that Paul had imposed on Bar-Jesus in Acts 13. The divine restraining order came in the form of a spirit of temporary blindness. A dark mist fell on their eyes and blindness overtook them and they started groping for support in the dark. Obviously, their sexual deviant nature didn't change but they were definitely restrained from violating Lot's daughters.

Life Application
S E C T I O N

Memory Verse

Many plans are in a man's mind, but it is the Lord's purpose for him that will stand (be carried out) (Proverbs 19:21 AMP).

Reflections

1. What is purpose?

2. Write down two purposes of divine restraining orders.

Chapter 10

Prayers of Activation: *Applying* DIVINE Restraining Orders Now

"Now, Lord, look on their threats, and grant to Your servants that with all boldness they may speak Your word, by stretching out Your hand to heal, and that signs and wonders may be done through the name of Your holy Servant Jesus." And when they had prayed, the place where they were assembled together was shaken; and they were all filled with the Holy Spirit, and they spoke the word of God with boldness.

— Acts 4:29-31

I T would be a mistake to close out a book such as this without giving you tools for activating divine restraining orders in your life. So this section of the book is going to focus on the different prayers of activation you can use to request or apply different types of divine restraining orders from the Courts of Heaven. Before we go into these prayers of activation, I want to talk briefly about the protocol for approaching the Courts of Heaven. All courts whether natural or spiritual are governed by judicial protocol. You will be better served by getting a copy of Robert Henderson's book, *Operating in the Courts of Heaven* to better understand the protocol of approaching the Courts of Heaven. However, the protocol that I present below will be sufficient to help you access different types of divine restraining orders. You can use the prayers of activation for yourself or you can have people you are praying for repeat the prayers after you.

Presenting Your Case

1. Get off the battlefield:

As Robert Henderson shares in his book:

> The first thing we must do to step into the courts of heaven is to get off the battlefield. We have to recognize the need for legal precedents to be set before we run to the battle. We are in a conflict, but it is a legal one. Remember that Jesus never pictures prayer in the battlefield context. He did put prayer however in a courtroom or judicial setting in Luke 18:1-8.[1]

2. Stand on Christ's finished work:

> *After this, Jesus, knowing that all things were now accom-*
> *plished, that the Scripture might be fulfilled, said, "I thirst!"*
> *Now a vessel full of sour wine was sitting there; and they*
> *filled a sponge with sour wine, put it on hyssop, and put it to*
> *His mouth. So when Jesus had received the sour wine, He*
> *said, "It is finished!" And bowing His head, He gave up His*
> *spirit* (John 19:28-30).

The second thing we must do is realize that approaching the Courts of Heaven must be based upon the finished work of Christ on the cross. Without this substitutionary work of our Savior, none of us qualify to approach the courts of a Holy God.

3. Repent:

The third thing we must do is realize before approaching the Courts of Heaven that we need to ask the Holy Spirit to search our hearts and see if there is any unconfessed sin in our life. It is very interesting to me that *repentance* is at the heart of entering the Kingdom. The introduction of the gospel of the Kingdom by both John the Baptist and Jesus was directly connected to the act of repenting.

> *From that time Jesus began to preach and to say, "Repent,*
> *for the kingdom of heaven is at hand"* (Matthew 4:17).

To "repent" means to *change your mind and reverse course*. Repentance resets your relationship with God and gives you a favorable standing in the Courts of Heaven. So it's quite sad when you hear some proponents of the "grace message" telling Christians they only need to repent once. As if born-again believers are incapable of sinning against God in this body of flesh.

4. Ask for the Court to be seated:

> *A fiery stream issued and came forth from before Him. A thousand thousands ministered to Him; ten thousand times ten thousand stood before Him. The court was seated, and the books were opened* (Daniel 7:10).

The fourth thing we must do before approaching the Courts of Heaven is ask that the Courts of Heaven be seated to hear our case. We make this request in and through the mighty name of Jesus Christ our Savior and Lord. It's impossible to get a judicial ruling from any court of law if the court is not yet seated. This is why no courtroom trial ever proceeds until the judge has been seated.

5. Present your case with boldness:

> *Let us therefore come boldly to the throne of grace, that we may obtain mercy and find grace to help in time of need* (Hebrews 4:16).

Boldness is an important spiritual ingredient for approaching the Throne of Grace. It demonstrates our confidence in the finished work of Christ and the goodness of God. When we approach the Courts of Heaven it's important that we do so in a spirit of boldness and not fear. Fear actually works against us and gives the devil legal footing against us in the Courts of Heaven. This is why the Bible says a person who fears is not perfected in the love of God (see 1 John 4:18).

6. Wait for the Spirit's witness:

*The Spirit Himself bears witness with our spirit that we are
children of God* (Romans 8:16).

One of the most important things we can do while we are presenting our case in the Courts of Heaven is wait for the witness of
the Holy Spirit before we leave the courtroom. As I stated earlier,
the Holy Spirit is the highest officer of the Courts of Heaven operating on earth today. He'll you give a witness in your spirit when the
divine restraining order you're seeking has been granted. If it has not
been granted, ask the Holy Spirit, "Why?" He's faithful to answer you
promptly, because all of Heaven wants to answer your prayers.

7. Receive the Court's verdict by faith:

*When Jesus had raised Himself up and saw no one but the
woman, He said to her, "Woman, where are those accusers
of yours? Has no one condemned you?" She said, "No one,
Lord." And Jesus said to her, "Neither do I condemn you;
go and sin no more"* (John 8:10-11).

No legal case inside any courtroom is ever considered complete
until a final verdict has been rendered. If a verdict has not been rendered, it may mean that the prosecutor has more evidence against the
plaintiff that the courts must also consider or the plaintiff's attorneys
have witness testimony or evidence on your behalf that they want the
courts to consider. This is why it's important for you to be persistent
until the Courts of Heaven have rendered a righteous verdict on your
behalf. The devil can only resist the Courts of Heaven from rendering
a righteous verdict on your behalf because he still has legal grounds

to do so. Ask the Holy Spirit to show you what is in Satan's evidence docket so you can render it useless. When your righteous verdict is rendered you must *receive it by faith.* This is because everything in the Kingdom of God is received by faith. You will not get a physical courier with a physical letter stating your righteous verdict. But believe me, a verdict rendered by the Courts of Heaven is more real and consequential than any verdict rendered by a natural court of law.

8. Reinforce your righteous verdict daily through thanksgiving:

One of the most powerful weapons in the Kingdom of God is *thanksgiving.* Thanksgiving places us in an attitude of continual praise over what the Lord has already done for us. Thanksgiving is so powerful that God has made it His direct will for all of His children. Thanksgiving feeds your spirit with hopeful anticipation. Thanksgiving feeds the spirit of expectancy inside of you. Miracles only happen in spiritual atmospheres charged with divine expectancy. Once the Holy Spirit gives you the "witness" that the *divine restraining order* you requested has been granted, it's important that you maintain an attitude of thanksgiving in the aftermath. *"In everything give thanks; for this is the will of God in Christ Jesus for you"* (1 Thess. 5:18).

Real-life Testimony

Before you start requesting divine restraining orders from the Courts of Heaven, there is a real-life testimony I want you to consider. This is a story of a woman who attended my church in Tempe (lovefestchurch.com), Arizona. She is a beautiful and godly woman who went through a devastating divorce with her husband in a marriage that produced two children. After their marriage ended her ex-husband became a little bit of a knucklehead with his new girlfriend. He was really harassing her and making it difficult for her to have custody of their children.

She came to me as her pastor to ask me what she could do. The constant fights were emotionally exhausting and nerve-wracking. She said to me, "Pastor, I don't know what to do. I am just so vexed."

"Would you like for us to bring your ex-husband before the Courts of Heaven and ask the Lord to impose a divine restraining order on his behavior?" I asked.

She had never heard of this concept before. She said to me, "What do you mean?"

"I am an officer of the Courts of Heaven. Give me his name and we will ask the Lord for a divine restraining order concerning his very abusive behavior toward you until there is a final injunction from the courts in Arizona on your custody battle." The woman and I went before the Courts of Heaven and asked for a divine restraining order. Within a week, God shut him down. Everything shifted. His abusive nature never changed, but he is no longer harassing her. It happened so quickly; the woman could hardly believe it. She hadn't been able to take her children out of the state for vacation. After we applied the divine restraining order he allowed her to take the children with her. Hallelujah!

Divine Restraining Orders versus the Spirit of Witchcraft

O foolish Galatians! Who has bewitched you that you should not obey the truth, before whose eyes Jesus Christ was clearly portrayed among you as crucified? (Galatians 3:1)

I have already stated the fact that divine restraining orders are an important aspect of *operating in the Courts of Heaven.* I've also established the legal precedence for both natural and spiritual restraining orders. Issuing divine restraining orders is one of the ways we can effectively and righteously resist the advancement of demonic entities against our life and destiny. However, there will be times when the Holy Spirit or the situation we are going through demand that we come before the Courts of Heaven to request a divine restraining order against another human being, like Paul applied one on Bar-Jesus (see Acts 13).

The Lord will not issue a divine restraining order against another human being if the person (child of God) asking for such an order from the Courts of Heaven is operating in a spirit of witchcraft. Witchcraft praying is when we use prayer to force other people to bend their free will in our favor instead of doing it for the glory of God. It is important I state this before we start releasing these "power packed" prayers of activation for issuing divine restraining orders. Are you ready? Let's get it "dun"!

Prayer of Repentance

If we say that we have no sin, we deceive ourselves, and the truth is not in us. If we confess our sins, He is faithful and just to forgive us our sins and to cleanse us from all unrighteousness (1 John 1:8-9).

I admonish you to pray the prayer of repentance below before you proceed to any of the *prayers of activation* for issuing divine restraining orders that follow this prayer of repentance. I once heard Brother Robert Henderson say, "Repenting several times will never hurt you spiritually before the Lord." In my Kingdom life experience, it's usually the lack of heartfelt repentance in the Body of Christ that's holding us back from experiencing the power of God more than the other way around.

Repeat this prayer loudly:

HEAVENLY FATHER, I approach the throne of grace in the name and through the blood of Jesus Christ, Your only begotten Son! Heavenly Father, Your Word says that if we confess our sins You are faithful and just to forgive our sin and cleanse us from all unrighteousness. Heavenly Father, I repent for every place I have disobeyed You concerning any restraining order You imposed upon my life. Lord, please forgive me! I repent for every time I have pressed through a restraining order of God and failed to obey Your word. I repent before You. I ask You to forgive me, and I ask that the case the enemy is presenting that says he has a legal right to hinder my destiny and to devour my life be rescinded in Jesus' name. I am repenting before You and I am asking You, Lord, to forgive me and to cause Satan's case against me in the Courts of Heaven to be silenced. May the blood of Jesus wash over me so the accuser of the brethren would not be able to speak against me. Lord, I ask that You give me another chance to live a life that's pleasing in Your eyes. Lord, I ask that You give me another chance even as You gave Samson another chance when his hair began to grow back. Heavenly Father, I ask that the blood of Jesus would speak on my behalf with regard to restraining orders that I need from You, Lord.

HEAVENLY FATHER, I ask that You would speak to me again. Give me a life-changing fresh word. I ask You to speak again in those places where I have violated restraining orders that You intended to govern my life and destiny. Lord, if You would speak again, I will obey You in Jesus' name I pray. Heavenly Father, I ask You to help me walk in the fear of the Lord. Help me not to treat Your holy Word lightly. Lord, I want to be among those who tremble at Your word, O God. Lord, I decree that I am forgiven in the name of Jesus. Thank You, Lord, for cleansing me from all unrighteousness. Heavenly Father, I repent of all known and unknown sin that the devil can use against me to try resist my spiritual breakthrough in the Courts of Heaven. In Jesus name, I pray. Amen!

Prayer #1

Divine Restraining Order against Premature Death

He shall call upon Me, and I will answer him; I will be with him in trouble; I will deliver him and honor him. With long life I will satisfy him, and show him My salvation (Psalm 91:15-16).

HEAVENLY FATHER, I stand in Your royal courtroom because of the blood and finished work of Jesus on the cross. I have come to receive Your righteous judgment over my life. Heavenly Father, I ask that the Courts of Heaven be seated according to Daniel 7:10. I ask this in Jesus' mighty name. Heavenly Father, I call upon Your holy angels to be witnesses to this legal and righteous transaction. I also decree and declare that all the demonic entities, institutions, and human beings who will be impacted directly by the divine restraining order that I am requesting will be duly notified by Your holy angels who service the Courts of Heaven, in Jesus' name I pray. Heavenly Father, I decree and declare that every demonic entity, earthly institution, and human being will respect, honor, and abide by Your righteous judgment, in Jesus' mighty name.

HEAVENLY FATHER, thank You for allowing me to stand before You and address the Courts of Heaven. Thank You, Lord, for the gift of revelation. Lord, I repent for any and everything that would be stopping my destiny from becoming a reality. Heavenly Father, even as I stand in your royal courtroom I present myself as a living sacrifice, holy and acceptable before You according to Romans 12:1. Lord, I ask that any place in me that is displeasing to You, that is unrighteous before You, would be unveiled so I can repent of it. O God, let the blood of Jesus speak on my behalf. Lord, I repent before You for any place of sin concerning wrong motives, wrong associations, or any place where I have not guarded my heart. Lord Jesus, I am sorry for my sins; cleanse me by Your blood so Satan has no legal footing to resist any divine restraining order I need from the Court. Heavenly Father, Your Word says that Jesus is my faithful Advocate before the Righteous Judge in the Courts of Heaven. Lord Jesus Christ, I summon You as my Advocate to help me plead my case before the Righteous Judge for a divine restraining order against any and all forms of premature death. Heavenly Father, I present before the Court the following scriptures as evidence against the spirit of premature death in my life.

It is written:

He shall call upon Me, and I will answer him; I will be with him in trouble; I will deliver him and honor him. With long life I will satisfy him, and show him My salvation (Psalm 91:15-16).

The thief does not come except to steal, and to kill, and to destroy. I have come that they may have life, and that they may have it more abundantly (John 10:10).

HEAVENLY FATHER, based upon the aforementioned scriptures, it is clear that premature death would do great injury to my life, destiny, and inflict irreparable damage to the purposes of God. Heavenly Father, I repent for my sin, my personal transgressions, and for the iniquities of my bloodline that may have opened a door for premature death in my life. In Jesus' name I pray. Lord, every sin of my forefathers that the enemy would be using as a legal right to build cases against me and to deny me my destiny, I ask that the blood of Jesus would just wash them away. It is written that a "Curse causeless would never arise." I ask that every legal right the spirit of premature death is holding on me to be revoked in Jesus' glorious name. Let the chains of the enemy be removed from my life.

HEAVENLY FATHER, I also repent for all covenants with demons that have existed in my ancestral bloodline. I am asking that every covenant with demonic powers will now be revoked and that their right to claim me and my bloodline would now be dismissed before Your Court, in Jesus' name. Thank You, Lord, for revoking these demonic covenants and altars in Jesus' mighty name! Heavenly Father, in my heartfelt desire to divorce myself from the spirit of premature death, I give back everything and anything that the devil would say came from his kingdom. I only want what the blood of Jesus has secured for me. So, I give back anything demons and demonic altars would claim that they have given me, in Jesus' name, I pray.

HEAVENLY FATHER, I now ask that a divine restraining order against premature death would be issued on my behalf from Your Supreme Court.

HEAVENLY FATHER, I decree and declare that any and all forms of premature-death plans the devil has issued or is orchestrating against my life are now cancelled in Jesus' glorious name. Heavenly Father, I receive this divine restraining order by faith, in Jesus' name. I decree and declare that You shall fulfill all "the days of my life" that You wrote in my book of destiny long before You created me. Amen!

Prayer #2

Divine Restraining Order against an Abusive Spouse

And this is the second thing you do: you cover the altar of the Lord with tears, with weeping and crying; so He does not regard the offering anymore, nor receive it with goodwill from your hands. Yet you say, "For what reason?" Because the Lord has been witness between you and the wife of your youth, with whom you have dealt treacherously; yet she is your companion and your wife by covenant (Malachi 2:13-14).

HEAVENLY FATHER, I stand in Your royal court-room because of the blood and finished work of Jesus on the cross. I have come to receive Your righteous judgment over my life. Heavenly Father' I ask that the Courts of Heaven be seated according to Daniel 7:10. I ask this in Jesus' mighty name. Heavenly Father, I call upon Your holy angels to be witnesses to this legal and righteous transaction. I also decree and declare that all the demonic entities, institutions, and human beings who will be impacted directly by the divine restraining order that I am requesting will be duly notified by Your holy angels who service the Courts of Heaven, in Jesus' name I pray. Heavenly Father, I decree and declare that every demonic entity, earthly institution, and human being will respect, honor, and abide by Your righteous judgment, in Jesus' mighty name.

HEAVENLY FATHER, I repent for any and everything that would be stopping my destiny from becoming a reality. Heavenly Father, even as I stand in the Court I present myself as a living sacrifice, holy and acceptable before You according to Romans 12:1. Lord, I repent before You for any place of sin concerning wrong motives, wrong intentions, or any place where I have not guarded my heart. Forgive me for letting evil thoughts and ideas cling to my mind. Lord Jesus, wash me with Your blood so Satan has no legal footing to resist any divine restraining order I need from Your Supreme Court.

HEAVENLY FATHER, Your Word says that Jesus is my faithful Advocate before the Righteous Judge in the Courts of Heaven. Lord Jesus Christ, I summon You as my Advocate to help me plead my case before the Righteous Judge for a divine restraining order against the pervasive, abusive, and violent behavior of my spouse or ex-spouse. Lord, it is not Your will for me to suffer emotional, sexual, or physical abuse in my life or marriage, in Jesus' name I pray.

HEAVENLY FATHER, I present before Your Supreme Court the following scriptures as evidence against the pervasive, abusive, and violent behavior of my spouse or ex-spouse.

It is written:

And this is the second thing you do: you cover the altar of the Lord with tears, with weeping and crying; so He does not regard the offering anymore, nor receive it with goodwill from your hands. Yet you say, "For what reason?" Because the Lord has been witness between you and the wife of your youth, with whom you have dealt treacherously; yet she is your companion and your wife by covenant (Malachi 2:13-14).

Do not envy the oppressor, and choose none of his ways (Proverbs 3:31).

HEAVENLY FATHER, based upon the aforementioned scriptures, it is clear that my spouse's or ex-spouse's abusive and violent behavior would do great injury to my life, destiny, and inflict irreparable damage to the purposes of God in my life. Heavenly Father, I repent for my sin, transgressions, and the iniquities of my bloodline that may have opened a door for the spirit of abuse in my life. In Jesus' name I pray. Lord, every sin of my forefathers that the enemy would be using as a legal right to build legal cases against me and to deny me my destiny, I ask that the blood of Jesus would just wash them away. I ask that every legal right the spirit of abuse is holding on me to is hereby revoked, in Jesus' glorious name.

HEAVENLY FATHER, I also repent for all covenants with demons that have existed in my ancestral blood-line. Lord, I ask that any agreement with demons that exist in my life would be rescinded. Lord, any demonic right to claim me and my bloodline is now dismissed before Your courts, in Jesus' name. Thank You, Lord, for revoking these demonic covenants and altars in Jesus' mighty name!

HEAVENLY FATHER, in my heartfelt desire to divorce myself from the spirit of abuse, I give back everything and anything that the devil would say came from his kingdom. I only want what the blood of Jesus secured for me on the cross. I give back anything demons and demonic altars would claim that they gave me.

HEAVENLY FATHER, I now ask that a divine restraining order against my abusive and violent spouse or ex-spouse be issued on my behalf by Your Royal and Supreme Court. In Jesus' name I pray. Heavenly Father, I decree and declare that any and all forms of abuse the devil is orchestrating against my life are now cancelled in Jesus' glorious name. Heavenly Father, I receive this divine restraining order by faith right now in Jesus' name. I decree and declare that You shall fulfill all "the days of my life" that You wrote in my book of destiny long before You created me, in Jesus' name I pray. Amen!

Prayer # 3

Divine Restraining Order
over Your Home

No evil shall befall you, nor shall any plague come near your dwelling; for He shall give His angels charge over you, to keep you in all your ways. In their hands they shall bear you up, lest you dash your foot against a stone (Psalm 91:10-12).

HEAVENLY FATHER, I stand in Your royal courtroom because of the shed blood and finished work of Jesus on the cross. I have come to receive Your righteous judgment over my life. Heavenly Father, I ask that the Courts of Heaven be seated according to Daniel 7:10. I ask this in Jesus' mighty name. Heavenly Father, I call upon Your holy angels to be witnesses to this legal and righteous transaction. I also decree and declare that all the demonic entities, institutions, and human beings who will be impacted directly by the divine restraining order that I am requesting will be duly notified by Your holy angels who service the Courts of Heaven, in Jesus' name I pray. Heavenly Father, I decree and declare that every demonic entity, earthly institution, and human being will respect, honor, and abide by Your righteous judgment, in Jesus' mighty name.

HEAVENLY FATHER, I repent for any and everything that would be stopping my destiny from becoming a reality. Heavenly Father, even as I stand in Your royal Courtroom I present myself as a living sacrifice, holy and acceptable before You according to Romans 12:1. Lord, I repent before You for any place of sin concerning wrong motives, wrong intentions, or any place where I have not guarded my heart. Forgive me for letting evil thoughts and ideas to cling to my mind. Lord Jesus, wash me with Your blood so Satan has no legal footing to resist any divine restraining order I need from Your Supreme Court.

HEAVENLY FATHER, Your Word says that Jesus is my faithful Advocate before the Righteous Judge in the Courts of Heaven. Lord Jesus Christ, I summon You as my Advocate to help me plead my case before the Righteous Judge for a divine restraining order over my home. Lord, it is not Your will for my home not to be a place of safety and peace against spiritual forces of darkness, in Jesus' name I pray.

HEAVENLY FATHER, I present before Your Court the following scriptures as evidence You should use to grant me a protective order over my home.

It is written:

No evil shall befall you, nor shall any plague come near your dwelling; for He shall give His angels charge over you, to keep you in all your ways. In their hands they shall bear you up, lest you dash your foot against a stone (Psalm 91:10-12).

The name of the Lord is a strong tower; the righteous run to it and are safe (Proverbs 18:10).

HEAVENLY FATHER, based upon the aforementioned scriptures, it is clear that if the Court does not impose a protective order over my home, the devil would cause great injury to my life, family, destiny, and inflict irreparable damage to the purposes of God. Heavenly Father, I repent for my sin, transgressions, and for the iniquities of my bloodline that may have opened a door for demons to attack the sanctity of my home. Lord, every sin of my forefathers that the devil is using as a legal right to build legal cases against me, to deny my destiny, I ask that the blood of Jesus would just wash them away. I ask that every legal right the devil has over my home be revoked, in Jesus' glorious name.

HEAVENLY FATHER, I also repent for any covenant with demons that has existed in my ancestral bloodline. Lord, I ask that any agreement with demons in my life would be rescinded. Lord, any demonic legal right to claim me, and my bloodline is now dismissed before Your royal court, in Jesus' name. Thank You, Lord, for revoking these demonic covenants and altars in Jesus' mighty name!

HEAVENLY FATHER, I divorce myself from all and any spirits of darkness that are after my home. I give back everything that the devil and demonic altars would say came from them. I only want what the blood of Jesus secured for me. Heavenly Father, I now ask that a divine restraining order against spiritual darkness be issued over my home by Your Royal and Supreme Court. In Jesus' name I pray. Heavenly Father, I decree and declare that any and all forms of spiritual attacks Satan is orchestrating against my home are now cancelled in Jesus' glorious name. Heavenly Father, I receive this divine restraining order by faith, in Jesus' name. I decree and declare that You shall fulfill all "the days of my life" that You wrote in my book of destiny long before You created me, in Jesus' name I pray. Amen!

Prayer #4

Divine Restraining Order over Your Church

Then the churches throughout all Judea, Galilee, and Samaria had peace and were edified. And walking in the fear of the Lord and in the comfort of the Holy Spirit, they were multiplied (Acts 9:31).

HEAVENLY FATHER, I stand in Your royal court-room because of the shed blood and finished work of Jesus on the cross. I have come to receive Your righteous judgment over my life. Heavenly Father, I ask that the Courts of Heaven be seated according to Daniel 7:10. I ask this in Jesus' mighty name. Heavenly Father, I call upon Your holy angels to be witnesses to this legal and righteous transaction. I also decree and declare that all the demonic entities, institutions, and human beings who will be impacted directly by the divine restraining order that I am requesting will be duly notified by Your holy angels who service the Courts of Heaven, in Jesus' name I pray. Heavenly Father, I decree and declare that every demonic entity, earthly institution, and human

being will respect, honor, and abide by Your righteous judgment, in Jesus' mighty name.

HEAVENLY FATHER, I repent for any and everything that would be stopping the destiny of our church from becoming a reality. Heavenly Father, even as I stand in your royal courtroom I present myself as a living sacrifice, holy and acceptable before You according to Romans 12:1. Lord, I repent before You for any place of sin concerning wrong motives, wrong intentions, or any place where I have not guarded my heart. Lord Jesus, wash me with Your blood so that Satan has no legal footing to resist any divine restraining order I need from Your Supreme Court concerning our church.

HEAVENLY FATHER, Your Word says that Jesus is my faithful Advocate before the Righteous Judge in the Courts of Heaven. Lord Jesus Christ, I summon You as my Advocate to help me plead my case before the Righteous Judge for a divine restraining order over our church. Lord, it is not Your will for our church not to be a place of safety and peace against spiritual forces of darkness, in Jesus' name I pray.

HEAVENLY FATHER, I present before Your Supreme Court the following scriptures as evidence as to why You should grant me a protective order over our church.

It is written:

Then the churches throughout all Judea, Galilee, and Samaria had peace and were edified. And walking in the fear of the Lord and in the comfort of the Holy Spirit, they were multiplied (Acts 9:31).

And I also say to you that you are Peter, and on this rock I will build My church, and the gates of Hades shall not prevail against it (Matthew 16:18).

HEAVENLY FATHER, based upon the aforementioned scriptures, it is clear that if the Court does not impose a restraining or protective order over our church and property, the devil could cause great injury to members of our church and inflict irreparable damage to the church's destiny. I ask that every legal right the devil has over our church be revoked in Jesus' glorious name. Heavenly Father, I also repent for any covenant with demons that has existed in my ancestral bloodline. Lord, I ask that any agreement with demons that my church has be rescinded. Lord, any demonic legal right to claim our church is now dismissed before Your royal courtroom, in Jesus' name. Thank You, Lord, for revoking these demonic covenants and altars in Jesus' mighty name!

HEAVENLY FATHER, I divorce myself and members of our congregation from spirits of darkness that are after our church. I give back everything that the devil, messengers of Satan and demonic altars would say came from them. I only want what the blood of Jesus secured for me on the cross. Heavenly Father, I now ask that a divine restraining order against spiritual forces be issued over our church by Your Royal and Supreme Court. In Jesus' name I pray. Heavenly Father, I decree and declare that any and all forms of spiritual attacks Satan is orchestrating against our church are now cancelled in Jesus' glorious name. Heavenly Father, I receive this divine restraining order by faith, in Jesus' name. Amen!

Prayer #5

Divine Restraining Order against Witchcraft

For there is no sorcery against Jacob, nor any divination against Israel. It now must be said of Jacob and of Israel, "Oh, what God has done!" (Numbers 23:23)

HEAVENLY FATHER, I stand in Your royal court-room because of the shed blood and finished work of Jesus on the cross. I have come to receive Your righteous judgment over my life. Heavenly Father, I ask that the Courts of Heaven be seated according to Daniel 7:10. I ask this in Jesus' mighty name. Heavenly Father, I call upon Your holy angels to be witnesses to this legal and righteous transaction. I also decree and declare that all the demonic entities, institutions, and human beings who will be impacted directly by the divine restraining order that I am requesting will be duly notified by Your holy angels who service the Courts of Heaven, in Jesus' name I pray. Heavenly Father, I decree and declare that every demonic entity, earthly institution, and human

being will respect, honor, and abide by Your righteous judgment, in Jesus' mighty name.

HEAVENLY FATHER, I repent for any and everything that would be stopping my destiny from becoming a reality. Heavenly Father, even as I stand in royal courtroom I present myself as a living sacrifice, holy and acceptable before You according to Romans 12:1. Lord, I repent before You for any place of sin concerning wrong motives, wrong intentions, or any place where I have not guarded my heart. Lord Jesus, wash me with Your blood so Satan has no legal footing to resist any divine restraining order I need from Your Supreme Court.

HEAVENLY FATHER, Your Word says that Jesus is my faithful Advocate before the Righteous Judge in the Courts of Heaven. Lord Jesus Christ, I summon You as my Advocate to help me plead my case before the Righteous Judge for a divine restraining order against any and all forms of witchcraft. Lord, it is not Your will for me to be harassed by the spirit of witchcraft, in Jesus' name I pray. Heavenly Father, I present before Your Supreme Court the following scriptures as evidence as to why You should grant me a divine restraining or protective order against any form of witchcraft.

It is written:

For there is no sorcery against Jacob, nor any divination against Israel. It now must be said of Jacob and of Israel, "Oh, what God has done!" (Numbers 23:23)

You shall not permit a sorceress to live (Exodus 22:18).

HEAVENLY FATHER, based upon the aforementioned scriptures, it is clear that if the Court does not impose a divine restraining order against the spirit of witchcraft on my behalf, the devil would cause great injury to my life, destiny, and inflict irreparable damage to the purposes of God. Heavenly Father, I repent for my sin, transgressions, and for the iniquities of my bloodline that opened a door for witchcraft to attack me. Lord, every sin of my forefathers that the enemy would be using as a legal right to build legal cases against me and to deny my destiny, I ask that the blood of Jesus would just wash them away. I ask that every legal right the devil has over my life be revoked, in Jesus' glorious name.

HEAVENLY FATHER, I also repent for any covenant with demons that has existed in my ancestral bloodline, especially with the spirit of witchcraft. Lord, I ask that any agreement with demons would be rescinded. Lord, any demonic legal right to claim me and my bloodline is now dismissed before Your courts, in Jesus' name. Thank You, Lord, for revoking these demonic covenants and altars in Jesus' mighty name!

HEAVENLY FATHER, I divorce myself from any and all forms of witchcraft that are after me. I give back everything that the devil, his messengers, and demonic altars would say came from them. I only want what the blood of Jesus secured for me on the cross. Heavenly Father, I now ask that a divine restraining order against witchcraft be issued over my life by Your

Supreme Court. In Jesus' name I pray. Heavenly Father, I decree that any and all forms of witchcraft that Satan is orchestrating against me are now cancelled in Jesus' glorious name. Heavenly Father, I receive this divine restraining order by faith, in Jesus' name. I decree and declare that You shall fulfill all "the days of my life" that You wrote in my book of destiny long before You created me, in Jesus' name I pray. Amen!

Prayer #6

Divine Restraining Order against Territorial Spirits

Assuredly, I say to you, whatever you bind on earth will be bound in heaven, and whatever you loose on earth will be loosed in heaven. Again I say to you that if two of you agree on earth concerning anything that they ask, it will be done for them by My Father in heaven (Matthew 18:18-19).

CAUTION: Pray this with a company of apostolic or prophetic leaders over your region.

HEAVENLY FATHER, we stand in Your royal court-room because of the shed blood and finished work of Jesus on the cross. As an apostolic council we have come to receive Your righteous judgment over this region. Heavenly Father, we ask that the Courts of

Heaven be seated according to Daniel 7:10. We ask this in Jesus' mighty name. Heavenly Father, we call upon Your holy angels to be witnesses to this legal and righteous transaction. We also decree and declare that all the demonic entities, institutions, and human beings who will be impacted directly by the divine restraining order that we are requesting will be duly notified by Your holy angels who service the Courts of Heaven, in Jesus' name we pray. Heavenly Father, we decree and declare that every demonic entity, earthly institution, and human being will respect, honor, and abide by Your righteous judgment, in Jesus' mighty name.

HEAVENLY FATHER, we repent for any and everything that would be stopping Your purpose for this region from becoming a reality. Heavenly Father, even as we stand in Your Supreme Court we present ourselves as a living sacrifice, holy and acceptable before You according to Romans 12:1. Lord, we repent before You for any place of sin concerning wrong motives, wrong intentions, or any place where we have not guarded our hearts as apostolic leaders in this region. Lord Jesus, wash us with Your blood so Satan has no legal footing to resist any divine restraining order we need from Your Supreme Court.

HEAVENLY FATHER, Your Word says that Jesus is our faithful Advocate before the Righteous Judge in the Courts of Heaven. Lord Jesus Christ, we summon You as our Advocate to help us plead our case before the Righteous Judge for a divine restraining order against any and all forms of territorial spirits that are holding the destiny of this region captive to the power of darkness. Lord, it is not Your will for this region to be covered in spiritual darkness, in Jesus' name we pray. Heavenly Father, we present before Your Supreme Court the following scriptures as evidence as to why You should grant us a divine restraining order against the territorial spirits that are operating over this region, for a period of time that the Holy Spirit will reveal to us.

It is written:

Assuredly, I say to you, whatever you bind on earth will be bound in heaven, and whatever you loose on earth will be loosed in heaven. Again I say to you that if two of you agree on earth concerning anything that they ask, it will be done for them by My Father in heaven (Matthew 18:18-19).

Unless the Lord builds the house, they labor in vain who build it; unless the Lord guards the city, the watchman stays awake in vain (Psalm 127:1).

HEAVENLY FATHER, based upon the aforementioned scriptures, it is clear that if the Court does not impose a divine restraining order against the territorial spirits that are holding this region captive, the devil will inflict irreparable damage to the purposes of God for this region. Heavenly Father, we repent for our sin and the transgressions of the Body of Christ in this region that may have opened doors for these territorial spirits to rule this region. Lord, every sin of city fathers, business, and political leaders that the enemy is using as a legal right to deny this region its God-given destiny, we ask that the blood of Jesus would just wash them away. We ask that every legal right the devil has over this region be revoked, in Jesus' glorious name.

HEAVENLY FATHER, we also repent for all covenants with demons that have existed throughout the history of this region. Lord, we ask that any agreement between demons and this region would be rescinded. Thank You, Lord, for revoking these demonic covenants and altars in Jesus' mighty name! Heavenly Father, representing the Body of Christ and the people of this region, we divorce ourselves from any and all territorial spirits that are ruling this region. On behalf of this region we give back everything in this region that the devil, his human messengers, and demonic altars would say came from them. We only want what the blood of Jesus has already secured for this region.

HEAVENLY FATHER, we now ask that a divine restraining order against these territorial spirits be issued over this region by Your Supreme Court. In Jesus' name we pray. Heavenly Father, we decree that any and all forms of demonic activity that Satan is orchestrating against this region are now cancelled in Jesus' glorious name. Heavenly Father, we receive this divine restraining order by faith, in Jesus' name. Amen!

Prayer #7

Divine Restraining Order against the Spirit of Poverty

The rich man's wealth is his strong city; the destruction of the poor is their poverty (Proverbs 10:15).

HEAVENLY FATHER, I stand in Your royal court-room because of the blood and finished work of Jesus on the cross. I have come to receive Your righteous judgment over my life. Heavenly Father, I ask that the Courts of Heaven be seated according to Daniel 7:10. I ask this in Jesus' mighty name. Heavenly Father, I call upon Your holy angels to be witnesses to this legal and righteous transaction. I also decree and declare that all the demonic entities, institutions, and human beings who will be impacted directly by the divine restraining order that I am requesting will be duly notified by Your holy angels who service the Courts of Heaven, in Jesus' name I pray. Heavenly Father, I decree and declare that every demonic entity, earthly institution, and human being will respect, honor, and abide by Your righteous judgment, in Jesus' mighty name.

HEAVENLY FATHER, I repent for any and every-thing that would be stopping my financial prosperity from becoming a reality. Heavenly Father, even as I stand in your royal courtroom I present myself as a liv-ing sacrifice, holy and acceptable before You according to Romans 12:1. Lord, I repent before You for any place of sin concerning wrong motives, wrong intentions, or any place where I have not guarded my heart. Lord Jesus, wash me with Your blood so Satan has no legal footing to resist any divine restraining order I need from Your Supreme Court.

HEAVENLY FATHER, Your Word says that Jesus is my faithful Advocate before the Righteous Judge in the Courts of Heaven. Lord Jesus Christ, I summon You as my Advocate to help me plead my case before the Righteous Judge for a divine restraining order against the spirit of poverty. I decree and declare that poverty's chokehold on my life is broken. Lord, it is not Your will for me to be poverty-stricken, in Jesus' name I pray. Heavenly Father, I present before Your Supreme Court the following scriptures as evidence as to why You should grant me a divine restraining order against the spirit of poverty.

It is written:

The rich man's wealth is his strong city; the destruction of the poor is their poverty (Proverbs 10:15).

For you know the grace of our Lord Jesus Christ, that though He was rich, yet for your sakes He became poor, that you through His poverty might become rich (2 Corinthians 8:9).

HEAVENLY FATHER, based upon the aforementioned scriptures, it is clear that if the Court does not impose a divine restraining order against the spirit of poverty controlling my life, the devil will cause great injury to my life, destiny, and inflict irreparable damage to the purposes of God. Heavenly Father, I repent for my sin, transgressions, and for the iniquities of my bloodline that opened a door for the spirit of poverty to afflict me. Lord, every sin of my forefathers that the devil is using as a legal right to build cases against me and to deny me financial prosperity, I ask that the blood of Jesus would just wash them away. I ask that every legal right the devil has over my life be revoked, in Jesus' glorious name.

HEAVENLY FATHER, I also repent for all covenants with demons that have existed in my ancestral bloodline. Lord, I ask that any agreement, any legal right the devil has to claim me and my bloodline is now dismissed before Your royal Court, in Jesus' name. Thank You, Lord, for revoking these demonic covenants and altars in Jesus' mighty name! Heavenly Father forgive me for times I have opened doors to the spirit of poverty by failing to give God my tithes of honor.

HEAVENLY FATHER, I divorce myself from the spirit of poverty and lack. I give back everything that the devil, his human messengers, and demonic altars would say came from them. I only want what the blood of Jesus secured for me. Heavenly Father, I now ask that a divine restraining order against the spirit of poverty be issued over my life by Your Supreme Court. In Jesus' name I pray. Heavenly Father, I decree that any and all forms of financial bankruptcy that Satan is orchestrating against me are now cancelled and made void in Jesus' glorious name. Heavenly Father, I receive this divine restraining order by faith, in Jesus' name.

I decree and declare that You shall fill my cup to over-flowing, in Jesus' name I pray. Amen!

Prayer #8

Divine Restraining Order against Familiar Spirits

The spirit of Egypt will fail in its midst; I will destroy their counsel, and they will consult the idols and the charmers, the mediums and the sorcerers (Isaiah 19:3).

HEAVENLY FATHER, I stand in Your royal court-room because of the shed blood and finished work of Jesus on the cross. I have come to receive Your righteous judgment over my life. Heavenly Father, I ask that the Courts of Heaven be seated according to Daniel 7:10. I ask this in Jesus' mighty name. Heavenly Father, I call upon Your holy angels to be witnesses to this legal and righteous transaction. I also decree and declare that all the demonic entities, institutions, and human beings who will be impacted directly by the divine restraining order that I am requesting will be duly notified by Your holy angels who service the Courts of Heaven, in Jesus' name I pray. Heavenly Father, I decree and declare that every demonic entity, earthly institution, and human being will respect, honor, and abide by Your righteous judgment, in Jesus' mighty name.

HEAVENLY FATHER, I repent for any and everything that would be stopping my destiny from becoming a reality. Heavenly Father, even as I stand in Your Supreme Court I present myself as a living sacrifice, holy and acceptable before You according to Romans 12:1. Lord, I repent before You for any place of sin concerning wrong motives, wrong intentions, or any place where I have not guarded my heart. Lord Jesus, wash me with Your blood so Satan has no legal footing to resist any divine restraining order I need from Your Supreme Court.

HEAVENLY FATHER, Your Word says that Jesus is my faithful Advocate before the Righteous Judge in the Courts of Heaven. Lord Jesus Christ, I summon You as my Advocate to help me plead my case before the Righteous Judge for a divine restraining order against any and all familiar spirits attached to my bloodline. Lord, it is not Your will for me to be harassed by generational curses and familiar spirits, in Jesus' name I pray. Heavenly Father, I present before Your Court the following scriptures as evidence why You should grant me a divine restraining order against any and all familiar spirits afflicting my life.

It is written:

The spirit of Egypt will fail in its midst; I will destroy their counsel, and they will consult the idols and the charmers, the mediums and the sorcerers (Isaiah 19:3).

And a slave does not abide in the house forever, but a son abides forever. Therefore if the Son makes you free, you shall be free indeed (John 8:35-36).

HEAVENLY FATHER, based upon the aforementioned scriptures, it is clear that if the Court does not impose a divine restraining order against these familiar spirits, the devil will cause great injury to my life, destiny, and inflict irreparable damage to the purposes of God. Heavenly Father, I repent for my sin, transgressions, and for the iniquities of my bloodline that may have opened a door for familiar spirits to attack me. Lord, every sin of my forefathers that the enemy would be using as a legal right to build cases against me and to deny my destiny, I ask that the blood of Jesus would just wash them away. I ask that every legal right the devil has over my life be revoked, in Jesus' glorious name.

HEAVENLY FATHER, I also repent for all covenants with demons that have existed in my ancestral bloodline. Lord, I ask that any agreement with demons would be rescinded. Lord, any demonic right to claim me and my bloodline is now dismissed before Your courts, in Jesus' name. Thank You, Lord, for revoking these demonic covenants and altars in Jesus' mighty name!

HEAVENLY FATHER, I divorce myself from any and all familiar spirits that are after me. I give back everything that the devil, his human messengers, and demonic altars would say came from them. I only want what the blood of Jesus secured for me. Heavenly Father, I now ask that a divine restraining order against familiar spirits be issued over my life by Your Supreme Court. In Jesus' name I pray. Heavenly Father, I decree that the power of any and all familiar spirits that Satan has assigned to me is now broken in Jesus' glorious name. Heavenly Father, I receive this divine restraining order by faith, in Jesus' name. Amen!

Prayer #9

Divine Restraining Order against Marriage Breakers

Therefore what God has joined together, let not man separate (Mark 10:9).

HEAVENLY FATHER, I stand in Your royal courtroom because of the blood and finished work of Jesus on the cross. I have come to receive Your righteous judgment over my life. Heavenly Father, I ask that the Courts of Heaven be seated according to Daniel 7:10. I ask this in Jesus' mighty name. Heavenly Father, I call upon Your holy angels to be witnesses to this legal and righteous transaction. I also decree and declare that all the demonic entities, institutions, and human beings who will be impacted directly by the divine restraining order that I am requesting will be duly notified by Your holy angels who service the Courts of Heaven, in Jesus' name I pray. Heavenly Father, I decree and declare that every demonic entity, earthly institution, and human being will respect, honor, and abide by Your righteous judgment, in Jesus' mighty name.

HEAVENLY FATHER, I repent for any and everything that would be stopping my marriage from becoming heaven here on earth. Heavenly Father, even as I stand in the Court I present myself as a living sacrifice, holy and acceptable before You according to Romans 12:1. Lord, I repent before You for any place of sin concerning wrong motives, wrong intentions, or any place where I have not guarded my heart. Lord Jesus, wash me with Your blood so Satan has no legal footing to resist any divine restraining order I need from Your Supreme Court.

HEAVENLY FATHER, Your Word says that Jesus is my faithful Advocate before the Righteous Judge in the Courts of Heaven. Lord Jesus Christ, I summon You as my Advocate to help me plead my case before the Righteous Judge for a divine restraining order against any and all marriage breakers. Lord, it is not Your will for my marriage to be harassed by spirits that destroy marriages, in Jesus' name I pray. Heavenly Father, I present before Your Supreme Court the following scriptures as evidence why You should grant me a divine restraining order against any and all marriage breakers.

It is written:

Therefore what God has joined together, let not man separate (Mark 10:9).

Marriage is honorable among all, and the bed undefiled; but fornicators and adulterers God will judge (Hebrews 13:4).

HEAVENLY FATHER, based upon the aforementioned scriptures, it is clear that if the Court does not impose a divine restraining order against these "marriage breakers" on my behalf, the devil will cause great injury to my life, destiny, and inflict irreparable damage to the purposes of God. Heavenly Father, I repent for my sin, transgressions, and for the iniquities of my bloodline that opened a door for these "marriage breakers" to attack my marriage. Lord, every sin of my forefathers that the enemy would be using as a legal right to build cases against me and to deny me a glorious marriage, I ask that the blood of Jesus would just wash them away. I ask that every legal right the devil has over my life be revoked, in Jesus' glorious name.

HEAVENLY FATHER, I also repent for all covenants with demons that have existed in my ancestral bloodline. Lord, I ask that any agreement with demons would be rescinded. Lord, any demonic right to claim me and my bloodline is now dismissed before Your courts, in Jesus' name. Thank You, Lord, for revoking these demonic covenants and altars in Jesus' mighty name!

HEAVENLY FATHER, I divorce myself from any and all "marriage breakers" that are after my marriage. I give back everything that the devil, messengers of satan, and demonic altars would say came from them. I only want what the blood of Jesus secured for me. Heavenly Father, I now ask that a divine restraining order against marriage breakers be issued over my life by Your Supreme Court. In Jesus' name I pray. Heavenly Father, I decree that all demonic spirits and agencies that Satan is orchestrating against me are now rendered powerless in Jesus' glorious name. Heavenly Father, I receive this divine restraining order by faith, in Jesus' name. Amen!

Prayer #10

Divine Restraining Order against Enemies of the Gospel

But Elymas the sorcerer (for so his name is translated) with-stood them, seeking to turn the proconsul away from the faith. Then Saul, who also is called Paul, filled with the Holy Spirit, looked intently at him and said, "O full of all deceit and all fraud, you son of the devil, you enemy of all righteousness, will you not cease perverting the straight ways of the Lord? And now, indeed, the hand of the Lord is upon you, and you shall be blind, not seeing the sun for a time" (Acts 13:8-11).

HEAVENLY FATHER, I stand in your royal court-room because of the blood and finished work of Jesus on the cross. I have come to receive Your righteous judgment over my life. Heavenly Father, I ask that the Courts of Heaven be seated according to Daniel 7:10. I ask this in Jesus' mighty name. Heavenly Father, I call upon Your holy angels to be witnesses to this legal and righteous transaction. I also decree and declare that all the demonic entities, institutions, and human beings who will be impacted directly by the divine restraining order that I am requesting will be duly notified by Your holy angels who service the Courts of Heaven, in Jesus' name I pray. Heavenly Father, I decree and declare that every demonic entity, earthly institution, and human being will respect, honor, and abide by Your righteous judgment, in Jesus' mighty name.

HEAVENLY FATHER, I repent for any and everything that would be stopping my destiny from becoming a reality. Heavenly Father, even as I stand in the Court I present myself as a living sacrifice, holy and acceptable before You according to Romans 12:1. Lord, I repent before You for any place of sin concerning wrong motives, wrong intentions, or any place where I have not guarded my heart. Lord Jesus, wash me with Your blood so Satan has no legal footing to resist any divine restraining order I need from Your Supreme Court.

HEAVENLY FATHER, Your Word says that Jesus is my faithful Advocate before the Righteous Judge in the Courts of Heaven. Lord Jesus Christ, I summon You as my Advocate to help me plead my case before the Righteous Judge for a divine restraining order against demonic and human entities who are enemies of the gospel in this region. Lord, it is not Your will for demonic spirits and wicked people to stop the further-ance of the gospel of Jesus Christ, in Jesus' name I pray. Heavenly Father, I present before Your Court the following scriptures as evidence why You should grant me a divine restraining order against any and all enemies of the gospel in this region, until I get an opportunity to preach the gospel to those who are ready for salvation.

It is written:

But Elymas the sorcerer (for so his name is translated) with-stood them, seeking to turn the proconsul away from the faith. Then Saul, who also is called Paul, filled with the Holy Spirit, looked intently at him and said, "O full of all deceit and all fraud, you son of the devil, you enemy of all righteousness, will you not cease perverting the straight ways of the Lord? And now, indeed, the hand of the Lord is upon you, and you shall be blind, not seeing the sun for a time" (Acts 13:8-11).

For I am not ashamed of the gospel of Christ, for it is the power of God to salvation for everyone who believes, for the Jew first and also for the Greek (Romans 1:16).

HEAVENLY FATHER, based upon the aforementioned scriptures, it is clear that if the Court does not impose a divine restraining order against the enemies of the gospel in this region, the devil will cause great hindrance to the furtherance of the gospel and inflict irreparable damage to the purposes of God. Heavenly Father, I repent for the sin, transgressions, and iniquities of the people in this region that may have opened a door for the devil to hinder the advancement of the gospel. Lord, concerning the cup of iniquity over this region that Satan is using as a legal right to resist the furtherance of the gospel, I ask that the blood of Jesus would just wash it away. I ask that every legal right the devil has over this region be revoked, in Jesus' glorious name.

HEAVENLY FATHER, I also repent for all covenants with demons that have existed in this region. Lord, I ask that any agreement with demons would be rescinded. Lord, any demonic right to claim this region is now dismissed before Your courts, in Jesus' name. Thank You, Lord, for revoking these demonic covenants and altars in Jesus' mighty name!

HEAVENLY FATHER, I divorce myself and this region from any and all forms of spiritual darkness. I give back everything that this region has received in the past that the devil, demons, and demonic altars would say came from them. Heavenly Father, I now ask that a divine restraining order against all enemies of the gospel be issued over this region by Your Supreme Court. In Jesus' name I pray. Heavenly Father, I decree that any and all forms of spiritual darkness that Satan is orchestrating against this region are now cancelled in Jesus' glorious name. Heavenly Father, I receive this divine restraining order by faith, in Jesus' name. I decree and declare that You shall fulfill the destiny of this region that You wrote in Your book of destiny long before You created this region, in Jesus' name I pray. Amen!

Prayer #11

Divine Restraining Order over Your Business/Career

Blessed shall be the fruit of your body, the produce of your ground and the increase of your herds, the increase of your cattle and the offspring of your flocks. Blessed shall be your basket and your kneading bowl (Deuteronomy 28:4-5).

HEAVENLY FATHER, I stand in Your royal court-room because of the blood and finished work of Jesus on the cross. I have come to receive Your righteous judgment over my life. Heavenly Father, I ask that the Courts of Heaven be seated according to Daniel 7:10. I ask this in Jesus' mighty name. Heavenly Father, I call upon Your holy angels to be witnesses to this legal and righteous transaction. I also decree and declare that all the demonic entities, institutions, and human beings who will be impacted directly by the divine restraining order that I am requesting will be duly notified by Your holy angels who service the Courts of Heaven, in Jesus' name I pray. Heavenly Father, I decree and declare that every demonic entity, earthly institution, and human being will respect, honor, and abide by Your righteous judgment, in Jesus' mighty name.

HEAVENLY FATHER, I repent for any and every-thing that would be stopping my business and career from prospering greatly. Heavenly Father, even as I stand in Your royal courtroom I present myself as a living sacrifice, holy and acceptable before You according to Romans 12:1. Lord, I repent before You for any place of sin concerning wrong motives, wrong intentions, or any place where I have not guarded my heart. Lord Jesus, wash me with Your blood so Satan has no legal footing to resist any divine restraining order I need from Your Supreme Court.

HEAVENLY FATHER, Your Word says that Jesus is my faithful Advocate before the Righteous Judge in the Courts of Heaven. Lord Jesus Christ, I summon You as my Advocate to help me plead my case before the Righteous Judge for a divine restraining order against any and all spirits of stagnation in my career and business. Lord, it is not Your will for me to remain stagnated in my career or business, in Jesus' name I pray. Heavenly Father, I present before Your Court the following scriptures as evidence why You should grant me a divine restraining order over my career and business against any form of stagnation.

It is written:

Blessed shall be the fruit of your body, the produce of your ground and the increase of your herds, the increase of your cattle and the offspring of your flocks. Blessed shall be your basket and your kneading bowl (Deuteronomy 28:4-5).

And the Lord will make you the head and not the tail; you shall be above only, and not be beneath, if you heed the commandments of the Lord your God, which I command you today, and are careful to observe them (Deuteronomy 28:13).

HEAVENLY FATHER, based upon the aforementioned scriptures, it is clear that if the Court does not impose a divine restraining order against spirits of stagnation in my life, the devil will cause great injury to my life, destiny, and inflict irreparable damage to the purposes of God. Heavenly Father, I repent for my sin, transgressions, and for the iniquities of my bloodline that opened a door for spirits of stagnation to afflict me. Lord, every sin of my forefathers that the enemy would be using as a legal right to build cases against me and to deny me my destiny, I ask that the blood of Jesus would just wash them away. I ask that every legal right the devil has over my life be revoked, in Jesus' glorious name.

HEAVENLY FATHER, I also repent for all covenants with demons that have existed in my ancestral bloodline. Lord, I ask that any agreement with demons would be rescinded. Lord, any demonic right to claim me and my bloodline is now dismissed before Your courts, in Jesus' name. Thank You, Lord, for revoking these demonic covenants and altars in Jesus' mighty name!

HEAVENLY FATHER, I divorce myself from any and all spirits of stagnation that are after me. I give back everything that the devil, demons, and demonic altars would say came from them. I only want what the blood of Jesus secured for me. Heavenly Father, I now ask that a divine restraining order against spirits of stagnation be issued over my life by Your Supreme Court. In Jesus' name I pray. Heavenly Father, I decree that any and all forms of stagnation that Satan is orchestrating against me are now cancelled in Jesus' glorious name. Heavenly Father, I receive this divine restraining order by faith, in Jesus' name. I decree and declare that You shall fulfill all the days of my life that You wrote in my book of destiny long before You created me, in Jesus' name I pray. Amen!

Prayer #12

Divine Restraining Order over Your Life

Then Jesus answered and said to them, "Most assuredly, I say to you, the Son can do nothing of Himself, but what He sees the Father do; for whatever He does, the Son also does in like manner" (John 5:19).

HEAVENLY FATHER, I stand in Your royal court-room because of the blood and finished work of Jesus on the cross. I have come to receive Your righteous judgment over my life. Heavenly Father, I ask that the Courts of Heaven be seated according to Daniel 7:10. I ask this in Jesus' mighty name. Heavenly Father, I call upon Your holy angels to be witnesses to this legal and righteous transaction. I also decree and declare that all the demonic entities, institutions, and human beings who will be impacted directly by the divine restraining order that I am requesting will be duly notified by Your holy angels who service the Courts of Heaven, in Jesus' name I pray. Heavenly Father, I decree and declare that every demonic entity, earthly institution, and human

being will respect, honor, and abide by Your righteous judgment, in Jesus' mighty name.

HEAVENLY FATHER, I repent for any and everything that would be stopping my destiny from becoming a reality. Heavenly Father, even as I stand in the Court I present myself as a living sacrifice, holy and acceptable before You according to Romans 12:1. Lord, I repent before You for any place of sin concerning wrong motives, wrong intentions, or any place where I have not guarded my heart. Lord Jesus, wash me with Your blood so Satan has no legal footing to resist any divine restraining order I need from Your Supreme Court.

HEAVENLY FATHER, Your Word says that Jesus is my faithful Advocate before the Righteous Judge in the Courts of Heaven. Lord Jesus Christ, I summon You as my Advocate to help me plead my case before the Righteous Judge for a divine restraining order over my life that will govern my God-given destiny. Lord, it is not Your will for me to do whatever I want, when I want, in Jesus' name I pray. Heavenly Father, I present before Your Court the following scriptures as evidence why You should show me the divine restraining order that You have placed over my life, to govern and order it.

It is written:

Then Jesus answered and said to them, "Most assuredly, I say to you, the Son can do nothing of Himself, but what He sees the Father do; for whatever He does, the Son also does in like manner" (John 5:19).

Father, if it is Your will, take this cup away from Me; nevertheless not My will, but Yours, be done" (Luke 22:42).

HEAVENLY FATHER, based upon the aforementioned scriptures, it is clear that if the Court does not impose a divine restraining order over my life, to govern and order it, the devil will cause great injury to my life, destiny, and inflict irreparable damage to the purposes of God by causing me to do my will instead of God's will. Heavenly Father, I repent for violating any divine restraining order You had previously placed upon my life. I ask that every legal right the devil has over my life be revoked, in Jesus' glorious name.

HEAVENLY FATHER, I also repent for all covenants with demons that have existed in my ancestral bloodline. Lord, I ask that any agreement with demons would be rescinded. Lord, any demonic right to claim me and my bloodline is now dismissed before Your courts, in Jesus' name. Thank You, Lord, for revoking these demonic covenants and altars in Jesus' mighty name!

HEAVENLY FATHER, I divorce myself from an independent spirit that is not submitted to God. I give back everything that the devil, demons, and demonic altars would say came from them. I only want what the blood of Jesus secured for me. Heavenly Father, I now ask that a divine restraining order be imposed on my life by Your Supreme Court. In Jesus' name I pray. Heavenly Father, I decree that any independent spirit over my life is now broken in Jesus' glorious name. Heavenly Father, I receive this divine restraining order by faith, in Jesus' name. I decree and declare that You shall fulfill all the days of my life that You wrote in my book of destiny long before You created me, in Jesus' name I pray. Amen!

Prayer #13

Divine Restraining Order over Your Piece of Land

"It shall be in that day," says the Lord of hosts, *"that I will cut off the names of the idols from the land, and they shall no longer be remembered. I will also cause the prophets and the unclean spirit to depart from the land"* (Zechariah 13:2).

HEAVENLY FATHER, I stand in Your royal courtroom because of the blood and finished work of Jesus on the cross. I have come to receive Your righteous judgment over my life. Heavenly Father, I ask that the Courts of Heaven be seated according to Daniel 7:10. I ask this in Jesus' mighty name. Heavenly Father, I call upon Your holy angels to be witnesses to this legal and righteous transaction. I also decree and declare that all the demonic entities, institutions, and human beings who will be impacted directly by the divine restraining order that I am requesting will be duly notified by Your holy angels who service the Courts of Heaven, in Jesus' name I pray. Heavenly Father, I decree and declare that every demonic entity, earthly institution, and human

being will respect, honor, and abide by Your righteous judgment, in Jesus' mighty name.

HEAVENLY FATHER, I repent for any sin or iniquity that is stopping prosperity on my piece of land. Heavenly Father, even as I stand in the Court I present myself as a living sacrifice, holy and acceptable before You according to Romans 12:1. Lord, I repent before You for any place of sin concerning wrong motives, wrong intentions, or any place where I have not guarded my heart. Lord Jesus, wash me with Your blood so Satan has no legal footing to resist any divine restraining order I need from Your Supreme Court.

HEAVENLY FATHER, Your Word says that Jesus is my faithful Advocate before the Righteous Judge in the Courts of Heaven. Lord Jesus Christ, I summon You as my Advocate to help me plead my case before the Righteous Judge for a divine restraining order over my piece of land, against forces of darkness. Lord, it is not Your will for my piece of land or real estate to be held in captivity to demonic powers and altars, in Jesus' name I pray. Heavenly Father, I present before Your Court the following scriptures as evidence as to why You should grant me a divine restraining order over my piece of land or real estate.

It is written:

"It shall be in that day," says the Lord of hosts, "that I will cut off the names of the idols from the land, and they shall no longer be remembered. I will also cause the prophets and the unclean spirit to depart from the land" (Zechariah 13:2).

If you are willing and obedient, you shall eat the good of the land (Isaiah 1:19).

HEAVENLY FATHER, based upon the aforementioned scriptures, it is clear that if the Court does not impose a divine restraining order over my piece of land or real estate against demonic invasion or barrenness, the devil will cause great injury to my life, destiny, and inflict irreparable damage to the purposes of God. Heavenly Father, I repent for any sin, transgressions, and iniquities that may have opened a door for demons to claim my piece of land or property. Lord, every sin of my forefathers that the enemy would be using as a legal right to build cases against me and to deny my destiny, I ask that the blood of Jesus would just wash them away. I ask that every legal right the devil has over my life be revoked, in Jesus' glorious name. Heavenly Father, I also repent for all covenants with demons that have existed in my ancestral bloodline. Lord, I ask that any agreement with demons would be rescinded. Lord, any demonic right to claim me and my land or property is now dismissed before Your Court, in Jesus' name. Thank You, Lord, for revoking these demonic covenants and altars in Jesus' mighty name!

HEAVENLY FATHER, I divorce myself from all idols and demonic spirits that are laying claim to my land. I give back everything that the devil, demons, and demonic altars would say came from them. I only want what the blood of Jesus secured for me. Heavenly Father, I now ask that a divine restraining order against demonic invasion or barrenness be issued over my piece of land by Your Supreme Court. In Jesus' name I pray. Heavenly Father, I decree that any curses and all forms of witchcraft that Satan is orchestrating against my piece of land or property are now cancelled in Jesus' glorious name. Heavenly Father, I receive this divine restraining order by faith, in Jesus' name. I decree and declare that You shall fulfill all the days of my life that You wrote in my book of destiny long before You created me, in Jesus' name I pray. Amen!

Prayer #14

Divine Restraining Order over Your Children

Then was fulfilled what was spoken by Jeremiah the prophet, saying: "A voice was heard in Ramah, lamentation, weeping, and great mourning, Rachel weeping for her children, refusing to be comforted, because they are no more" (Matthew 2:17-18).

HEAVENLY FATHER, I stand in Your royal courtroom because of the blood and finished work of Jesus on the cross. I have come to receive Your righteous judgment over my life. Heavenly Father, I ask that the Courts of Heaven be seated according to Daniel 7:10. I ask this in Jesus' mighty name. Heavenly Father, I call upon Your holy angels to be witnesses to this legal and righteous transaction. I also decree and declare that all the demonic entities, institutions, and human beings who will be impacted directly by the divine restraining order that I am requesting will be duly notified by Your holy angels who service the Courts of Heaven, in Jesus' name I pray. Heavenly Father, I decree and declare that every demonic entity, earthly institution, and human being will respect, honor, and abide by Your righteous judgment, in Jesus' mighty name.

HEAVENLY FATHER, I repent for any and everything that is stopping the destinies of my children from becoming a reality. Heavenly Father, even as I stand in Your royal courtroom I present myself as a living sacrifice, holy and acceptable before You according to Romans 12:1. Lord, I repent before You for any place of sin concerning wrong motives, wrong intentions, or any place where I have not guarded my heart. Lord Jesus, wash me with Your blood so Satan has no legal footing to resist any divine restraining order I need from Your Supreme Court.

HEAVENLY FATHER, Your Word says that Jesus is my faithful Advocate before the Righteous Judge in the Courts of Heaven. Lord Jesus Christ, I summon You as my Advocate to help me plead my case before the Righteous Judge for a divine restraining order over my children against all demonic devices against them. Lord, it is not Your will for my children to be harassed or led astray by demonic spirits, in Jesus' name I pray. Heavenly Father, I present before Your Court the following scriptures as evidence why You should grant me a protective order over my children.

It is written:

Then was fulfilled what was spoken by Jeremiah the prophet, saying: "A voice was heard in Ramah, lamentation, weeping, and great mourning, Rachel weeping for her children, refusing to be comforted, because they are no more" (Matthew 2:17-18).

Behold, children are a heritage from the Lord, the fruit of the womb is a reward. Like arrows in the hand of a warrior, so are the children of one's youth (Psalm 127:3-4).

HEAVENLY FATHER, based upon the aforementioned scriptures, it is clear that if the Court does not impose a divine restraining order over my children to protect them against Satan's diabolical assignments, the devil will cause great injury to my children's lives, destiny, and inflict irreparable damage to the purposes of God. Heavenly Father, I repent for my sin, transgressions, and for the iniquities of my bloodline that may have opened a door for the devil to attack my children. Lord, every sin of my forefathers that the devil is using as a legal right to build cases against me and to deny my destiny, I ask that the blood of Jesus would just wash them away. I ask that every legal right the devil has over my life be revoked, in Jesus' glorious name.

HEAVENLY FATHER, I also repent for all covenants with demons that have existed in my ancestral bloodline. Lord, I ask that any agreement with demons would be rescinded. Lord, any demonic right to claim me and my bloodline is now dismissed before Your courts, in Jesus' name. Thank You, Lord, for revoking these demonic covenants and altars in Jesus' mighty name!

HEAVENLY FATHER, I divorce my children from any and all forms of demonic entities that are after them. I give back everything that the devil, his human messengers, and demonic altars would say came from them. I only want what the blood of Jesus secured for my children. Heavenly Father, I now ask that a divine restraining order over my children be issued immediately by Your Supreme Court. In Jesus' name I pray. Heavenly Father, I decree that any and all forms of tactics that Satan is orchestrating against my children are now cancelled in Jesus' glorious name. Heavenly Father, I receive this divine restraining order by faith, in Jesus' name. I decree and declare that You shall fulfill all the days of my children's life that You wrote in their book of destiny long before You created them, in Jesus' name I pray. Amen!

Prayer #15

Divine Restraining Order against Acts of Terrorism

You shall not be afraid of the terror by night, nor of the arrow that flies by day, nor of the pestilence that walks in darkness, nor of the destruction that lays waste at noonday (Psalm 91:5-6).

HEAVENLY FATHER, I stand in Your royal courtroom because of the blood and finished work of Jesus on the cross. I have come to receive Your righteous judgment over my life. Heavenly Father, I ask that the Courts of Heaven be seated according to Daniel 7:10. I ask this in Jesus' mighty name. Heavenly Father, I call upon Your holy angels to be witnesses to this legal and righteous transaction. I also decree and declare that all the demonic entities, institutions, and human beings who will be impacted directly by the divine restraining order that I am requesting will be duly notified by Your holy angels who service the Courts of Heaven, in Jesus' name I pray. Heavenly Father, I decree and declare that every demonic entity, earthly institution, and human being will respect, honor, and abide by Your righteous judgment, in Jesus' mighty name.

HEAVENLY FATHER, I repent for any and everything that would make my city or me be a victim of terrorism. Heavenly Father, even as I stand in the Court I present myself as a living sacrifice, holy and acceptable before You according to Romans 12:1. Lord, I repent before You for any place of sin concerning wrong motives, wrong intentions, or any place where I have not guarded my heart. Lord Jesus, wash me with Your blood so Satan has no legal footing to resist any divine restraining order I need from Your Supreme Court.

HEAVENLY FATHER, Your Word says that Jesus is my faithful Advocate before the Righteous Judge in the Courts of Heaven. Lord Jesus Christ, I summon You as my Advocate to help me plead my case before the Righteous Judge for a divine restraining order against any and all forms of terrorism. Lord, it is not Your will for me or the people in my city to be harassed by the spirit of terrorism, in Jesus' name I pray. Heavenly Father,

I present before Your Supreme Court the following scriptures as evidence as to why You should grant me a divine restraining order against any and all forms of terrorism within one mile from me.

It is written:

You shall not be afraid of the terror by night, nor of the arrow that flies by day, nor of the pestilence that walks in darkness, nor of the destruction that lays waste at noonday (Psalm 91:5-6).

"No weapon formed against you shall prosper, and every tongue which rises against you in judgment you shall condemn. This is the heritage of the servants of the Lord, and their righteousness is from Me," says the Lord (Isaiah 54:17).

HEAVENLY FATHER, based upon the aforementioned scriptures, it is clear that if the Court does not impose a divine restraining order against the spirit of terrorism, the devil will cause great injury to my life, my city, and also inflict irreparable damage to the purposes of God. Heavenly Father, I repent for the sin, transgressions, and iniquities of my city that opened a door for the spirit of terrorism to attack us. Lord, everything that the enemy would use as legal grounds for building cases against me and my city to deny our God-given destiny, I ask that the blood of Jesus would just wash them away. I ask that every legal right the devil has over my life be revoked, in Jesus' glorious name.

HEAVENLY FATHER, I also repent for all covenants with demons that have existed in the history of my city. Lord, I ask that any agreement with demons would be rescinded. Lord, any demonic right to claim me and my bloodline is now dismissed before Your courts, in Jesus' name. Thank You, Lord, for revoking these demonic covenants and altars in Jesus' mighty name!

HEAVENLY FATHER, I divorce myself and the city I live in from any and all forms of terrorism. Lord, on behalf of my city and myself I give back everything that the devil, demons, and demonic altars would say came from them. I only want what the blood of Jesus secured for my city and me. Heavenly Father, I now ask that a divine restraining order against terrorism be issued over my life and over my city by Your Supreme Court. In Jesus' name I pray. Heavenly Father, I decree that any and all forms of terrorism that Satan is orchestrating against me and the city I live in are now cancelled in Jesus' glorious name. Heavenly Father, I receive this divine restraining order by faith, in Jesus' name. I decree and declare that You shall fulfill all the days of my life that You wrote in my book of destiny long before You created me, in Jesus' name I pray. Amen!

Prayer #16

Divine Restraining Order against Devastating Storms

Then the Lord will create above every dwelling place of Mount Zion, and above her assemblies, a cloud and smoke by day and the shining of a flaming fire by night. For over all the glory there will be a covering. And there will be a tabernacle for shade in the daytime from the heat, for a place of refuge, and for a shelter from storm and rain (Isaiah 4:5-6).

HEAVENLY FATHER, I stand in Your royal courtroom because of the blood and finished work of Jesus on the cross. I have come to receive Your righteous judgment over my life. Heavenly Father, I ask that the Courts of Heaven be seated according to Daniel 7:10. I ask this in Jesus' mighty name. Heavenly Father, I call upon Your holy angels to be witnesses to this legal and righteous transaction. I also decree and declare that all the demonic entities, institutions, and human beings who will be impacted directly by the divine restraining order that I am requesting will be duly notified by Your holy angels who service the Courts of Heaven, I pray. Heavenly Father, I decree and declare that every demonic entity, earthly institution, and human being will respect, honor, and abide by Your righteous judgment, in Jesus' mighty name.

HEAVENLY FATHER, on behalf of the people in my city and state, I repent for any and everything that we have done that opened the door to devastating storms on our city or state. Heavenly Father, even as I stand in the Court I present myself as a living sacrifice, holy and acceptable before You according to Romans 12:1. Lord, I repent before You for any place of sin concerning wrong motives, wrong intentions, or any place where I have not guarded my heart. Lord Jesus, wash me with Your blood so Satan has no legal footing to resist any divine restraining order I need from Your Supreme Court.

HEAVENLY FATHER, Your Word says that Jesus is my faithful Advocate before the Righteous Judge in the Courts of Heaven. Lord Jesus Christ, I summon You as my Advocate to help me plead my case before the Righteous Judge for a divine restraining order against any and all forms of devastating storms and hurricanes. Lord, it is not Your will for me and this city or state to be destroyed by demonically engineered storms and hurricanes, in Jesus' name I pray. Heavenly Father, I present before Your Court the following scriptures as evidence why You should grant me and my city or state a divine restraining order against these demonically engineered storms and hurricanes.

It is written:

Then the Lord will create above every dwelling place of Mount Zion, and above her assemblies, a cloud and smoke by day and the shining of a flaming fire by night. For over all the glory there will be a covering. And there will be a tabernacle for shade in the daytime from the heat, for a place of refuge, and for a shelter from storm and rain (Isaiah 4:5-6).

Then He arose and rebuked the wind, and said to the sea, "Peace, be still!" And the wind ceased and there was a great calm (Mark 4:39).

HEAVENLY FATHER, based upon the aforementioned scriptures, it is clear that if the Court does not impose a divine restraining order against these demonically engineered storms and hurricanes, the devil will cause great injury to my life, property, and inflict irreparable damage to the purposes of God. Heavenly Father, I repent on behalf of my city or state for our sin, transgressions, and iniquities that may have opened a door for these demonically engineered storms and hurricanes to attack us. Lord, forgive the sin of my city or state that the devil is using as a legal foothold against my city or state in order to destroy my city or state; I ask that the blood of Jesus would just wash it away. I ask that every legal right the devil has over my city or state be revoked, in Jesus' glorious name.

HEAVENLY FATHER, I also repent for all covenants with demons that have existed in my city or state's history. Lord, I ask that any agreement with demons would be rescinded. Lord, any demonic right to claim me and my bloodline is now dismissed before Your courts, in Jesus' name. Thank You, Lord, for revoking these demonic covenants and altars in Jesus' mighty name! Heavenly Father, I divorce myself and my city and state from any and all iniquities that Satan is standing on.

On behalf of my city or state I give back everything that the devil, demons, and demonic altars would say came from them. I only want what the blood of Jesus secured for me and my city or state. Heavenly Father, I now ask that a divine restraining order against demonically engineered storms and hurricanes be issued immediately by Your Supreme Court. In Jesus' name I pray. Heavenly Father, I decree that any and all forms of storms and hurricanes that Satan is orchestrating against my city or state are now cancelled in Jesus' glorious name. Heavenly Father, I receive this divine restraining order by faith, in Jesus' name. I decree and declare that You shall fulfill all the days of my life that You wrote in my book of destiny long before You created me, in Jesus' name I pray. Amen!

Prayer #17

Divine Restraining Order against Demonic Dreams

And the king said to them, "I have had a dream, and my spirit is anxious to know the dream" (Daniel 2:3).

HEAVENLY FATHER, I stand in Your royal courtroom because of the blood and finished work of Jesus on the cross. I have come to receive Your righteous judgment over my life. Heavenly Father, I ask that the Courts of Heaven be seated according to Daniel 7:10. I ask this in Jesus' mighty name. Heavenly Father, I call upon Your holy angels to be witnesses to this legal and righteous transaction. I also decree and declare that all the demonic entities, institutions, and human beings who will be impacted directly by the divine restraining order that I am requesting will be duly notified by Your holy angels who service the Courts of Heaven, in Jesus' name I pray. Heavenly Father, I decree and declare that every demonic entity, earthly institution, and human being will respect, honor, and abide by Your righteous judgment, in Jesus' mighty name.

HEAVENLY FATHER, I repent for any and everything that Satan is using to visit demonic dreams upon me while stopping my destiny from becoming a reality. Heavenly Father, even as I stand in Your Court I present myself as a living sacrifice, holy and acceptable before You according to Romans 12:1. Lord, I repent before You for any place of sin concerning wrong motives, wrong intentions, or any place where I have not guarded my heart. Lord Jesus, wash me with Your blood so Satan has no legal footing to resist any divine restraining order I need from Your Supreme Court.

HEAVENLY FATHER, Your Word says that Jesus is my faithful Advocate before the Righteous Judge in the Courts of Heaven. Lord Jesus Christ, I summon You as my Advocate to help me plead my case before the Righteous Judge for a divine restraining order against any and all forms of demonically engineered dreams. Lord, it is not Your will for me to be harassed by night-mares or demonic dreams, in Jesus' name I pray. Heavenly Father, I present before Your Supreme Court the following scriptures as evidence as to why You should grant me a divine restraining order against any and all forms of demonically engineered dreams.

It is written:

And the king said to them, "I have had a dream, and my spirit is anxious to know the dream" (Daniel 2:3).

For God may speak in one way, or in another, yet man does not perceive it. In a dream, in a vision of the night, when deep sleep falls upon men, while slumbering on their beds (Job 33:14-15).

HEAVENLY FATHER, based upon the aforementioned scriptures, it is clear that if the Court does not impose a divine restraining order against demonically engineered dreams in my life, the devil will cause great injury to my life, destiny, and inflict irreparable damage to the purposes of God. Heavenly Father, I repent for my sin, transgressions, and for the iniquities of my bloodline that may have opened a door for demonically engineered dreams to afflict me. Lord, every sin of my forefathers that the enemy would be using as a legal right to build cases against me and to deny me my destiny, I ask that the blood of Jesus would just wash it away. I ask that every legal right the devil has over my life be revoked, in Jesus' glorious name. Heavenly Father, I also repent for all covenants with demons that have existed in my ancestral bloodline. Lord, I ask that any agreement with demons would be rescinded. Lord, any demonic right to claim my bloodline and me is now dismissed before Your courts, in Jesus' name. Thank

You, Lord, for revoking these demonic covenants and altars in Jesus' mighty name!

HEAVENLY FATHER, I divorce myself from any and all forms of demonically engineered dreams and nightmares that have afflicted me. I give back everything that the devil, demons, and demonic altars would say came from them. I only want what the blood of Jesus secured for me. Heavenly Father, I now ask that a divine restraining order against demonically engineered dreams and nightmares be issued over my life by Your Supreme Court. In Jesus' name I pray. Heavenly Father, I decree that any and all forms of demonically engineered dreams that Satan is using against me are now cancelled in Jesus' glorious name. Heavenly Father, I receive this divine restraining order by faith, in Jesus' name. I decree and declare that You shall fulfill all the days of my life that You wrote in my book of destiny long before You created me, in Jesus' name I pray. Amen!

Prayer #18

Divine Restraining Order against Destiny Killers

Now when they had departed, behold, an angel of the Lord appeared to Joseph in a dream, saying, "Arise, take the young Child and His mother, flee to Egypt, and stay there until I bring you word; for Herod will seek the young Child to destroy Him" (Matthew 2:13).

HEAVENLY FATHER, I stand in Your royal court-room because of the blood and finished work of Jesus on the cross. I have come to receive Your righteous judgment over my life. Heavenly Father, I ask that the Courts of Heaven be seated according to Daniel 7:10. I ask this in Jesus' mighty name. Heavenly Father, I call upon Your holy angels to be witnesses to this legal and righteous transaction. I also decree and declare that all the demonic entities, institutions, and human beings who will be impacted directly by the divine restraining order that I am requesting will be duly notified by Your holy angels who service the Courts of Heaven, in Jesus' name I pray. Heavenly Father, I decree and declare that every demonic entity, earthly institution, and human being will respect, honor, and abide by Your righteous judgment, in Jesus' mighty name.

HEAVENLY FATHER, I repent for any and every-thing that has empowered the army of destiny killers against me and is stopping my destiny from becom-ing a reality. Heavenly Father, even as I stand in Your royal courtroom I present myself as a living sacrifice, holy and acceptable before You according to Romans 12:1. Lord, I repent before You for any place of sin con-cerning wrong motives, wrong intentions, or any place where I have not guarded my heart. Lord Jesus, wash me with Your blood so Satan has no legal footing to resist any divine restraining order I need from Your Supreme Court.

HEAVENLY FATHER, Your Word says that Jesus is my faithful Advocate before the Righteous Judge in the Courts of Heaven. Lord Jesus Christ, I summon You as my Advocate to help me plead my case before the Righteous Judge for a divine restraining order against any and all forms of destiny killers. Lord, it is not Your will for me to be harassed by an army of destiny killers, in Jesus' name I pray. Heavenly Father, I present before Your Supreme Court the following scriptures as evidence why You should grant me a divine restraining order against the army of destiny killers.

It is written:

Now when they had departed, behold, an angel of the Lord appeared to Joseph in a dream, saying, "Arise, take the young Child and His mother, flee to Egypt, and stay there until I bring you word; for Herod will seek the young Child to destroy Him" (Matthew 2:13).

And we know that all things work together for good to those who love God, to those who are the called according to His purpose (Romans 8:28).

HEAVENLY FATHER, based upon the aforementioned scriptures, it is clear that if the Court does not impose a divine restraining order against the army of destiny killers that are working against me, the devil will cause great injury to my life, God-given destiny, and also inflict irreparable damage to the purposes of God. Heavenly Father, I repent for my sin, transgressions, and for the iniquities of my bloodline that opened a door for the army of destiny killers to attack me. Lord, every sin of my forefathers that the enemy would be using as a legal right to build cases against me and to deny me my destiny, I ask that the blood of Jesus would just wash it away. I ask that every legal right the devil has over my life be revoked, in Jesus' glorious name.

HEAVENLY FATHER, I also repent for all covenants with demons that have existed in my ancestral bloodline. Lord, I ask that any agreement with demons would be rescinded. Lord, any demonic right to claim my bloodline and me is now dismissed before Your courts, in Jesus' name. Thank You, Lord, for revoking these demonic covenants and altars in Jesus' mighty name!

HEAVENLY FATHER, I divorce myself from the army of destiny killers that is after me. I give back everything that the devil, demons, and demonic altars would say came from them. I only want what the blood of Jesus secured for me. Heavenly Father, I now ask that a divine restraining order against the army of destiny killers be issued over my life by Your Supreme Court. In Jesus' name I pray. Heavenly Father, I decree that any and all forms of destiny killers that Satan is orchestrating against me are now cancelled in Jesus' glorious name. Heavenly Father, I receive this divine restraining order by faith, in Jesus' name. I decree and declare that You shall fulfill all the days of my life that You wrote in my book of destiny long before You created me, in Jesus' name I pray. Amen!

Endnotes

Chapter 1
Operating from the Heavenly Courtroom

1. "Restraining Order," Wikipedia, February 28, 2019, https:// en.wikipedia.org/wiki/Restraining_order.

Chapter 3
Understanding Divine Restraining Orders

1. Ibid.

Chapter 7
Features of a Divine Restraining Order

1. West's Encyclopedia of American Law, second ed., s.v. "restraining orders," accessed March 14, 2019, https://legal -dictionary.thefreedictionary.com/restraining+orders.

Chapter 10
Prayers of Activation: Applying Divine Restraining Orders Now

1. Robert Henderson, *Operating in the Courts of Heaven* (Shippensburg, PA: Destiny Image, 2016).

Notes

About

Dr. Francis Myles

D R. Francis Myles is a multi-gifted international motivational speaker, business consultant, and apostle to the nations. Senior pastor of Lovefest Church International in Tempe, Arizona and Lusaka, Zambia, he is also the creator and founder of the world's first Marketplace Bible™. He is a sought after conference speaker in both ministerial and marketplace seminars. He is also a spiritual life coach to movers and shakers in the marketplace and political arena. He has appeared on TBN, GodTV, and Daystar. He has been a featured guest on Sid Roth's *It's Supernatural!* TV show and *This Is Your Day* with Pastor Benny Hinn. He is happily married to the love of his life, Carmela Real Myles, and they reside in Scottsdale in the state of Arizona.

About

Robert Henderson

ROBERT Henderson is a global apostolic leader who operates in revelation and impartation. His teaching empowers the Body of Christ to see the hidden truths of Scripture clearly and apply them for breakthrough results. Driven by a mandate to disciple nations through writing and speaking, Robert travels extensively around the globe, teaching on the apostolic, the Kingdom of God, the "Seven Mountains," and most notably, the Courts of Heaven. He has been married to Mary for 40 years. They have six children and five grandchildren. Together they are enjoying life in beautiful Midlothian, Texas.

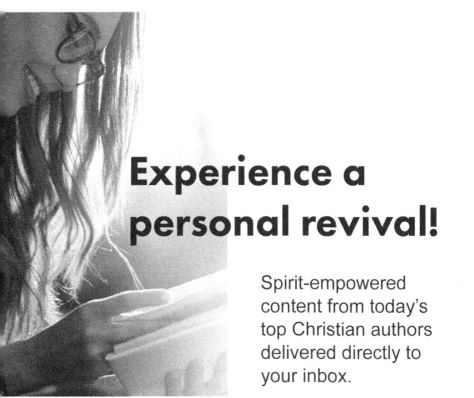

Experience a personal revival!

Spirit-empowered content from today's top Christian authors delivered directly to your inbox.

Inspiring Articles
Powerful Video Teaching
Resources for Revival

Get all of this and so much more, e-mailed to you twice weekly!

LOVE TO READ CLUB
by **D DESTINY IMAGE**

Made in the USA
Monee, IL
14 April 2020